SPORT AND POLITICS

SPORT AND POLITICS

The Olympics and the Los Angeles Games

Bill Shaikin

WITHDRAWN

PRAEGER

New York
Westport, Connecticut
London

Library of Congress Cataloging-in-Publication Data

Shaikin, Bill.
  Sport and politics.

  Bibliography: p.
  Includes index.
  1. Olympic games (23rd : 1984 : Los Angeles, Calif.)—
Political aspects. 2. Olympic games—Political aspects—
Case studies. 3. Sports and state—Case studies.
I. Title.
GV722 1984.S42 1988   796.4'8   87-17660
ISBN 0-275-92786-5 (alk. paper)

Library of Congress Catalog Card Number: 87-17660
ISBN: 0-275-92786-5

First published in 1988

Praeger Publishers, One Madison Avenue, New York, NY 10010
A division of Greenwood Press, Inc.

Printed in the United States of America

The paper used in this book complies with the
Permanent Paper Standard issued by the National
Information Standards Organization (Z39.48-1984).

10 9 8 7 6 5 4 3 2 1

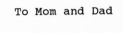
To Mom and Dad

Contents

Preface

Politics have nothing to do with sport.
Zola Budd, Olympic runner

To Zola Budd, the Olympic Games were strictly a sporting event. The 17-year-old girl viewed herself as a world-class runner and the Olympics as a world-class competition. Therefore, Budd reasoned, she should participate in the Games. The logic was simple to Budd--and simplistic to seasoned Olympic observers. Budd's belief is at best naive and at worst dangerous. The Budd episode is discussed in Chapter Three, but suffice it to say here that she was viewed throughout the world as a South African woman, not an innocent little girl, trying to take part in an event where the political competition rivals--and often overshadows--the athletic competition.

The core of this work examines the politics of the 1984 Los Angeles Olympics, in which the Budd affair played a small but important part. The analysis will be clearest if the reader is familiar with the sporting and political contexts in which the Los Angeles Games were set.

Many people share Zola Budd's beliefs, and Chapter One devotes itself to dispelling that fanciful notion. The chapter provides a brief introduction to sport and politics, and it illuminates the links between them. Chapter One takes many of its examples from U.S. society, a cultural context likely to be familiar to most readers.

Chapter Two highlights the history of politics in the Olympics. The chapter employs a thematic, not a chronological, approach. Its goal is to allow an appreciation of the great extent to which politics has always been intertwined with the Olympic Games, rather than to provide a comprehensive chronicle of that enduring mix. Readers will discover that politics has been a part of the Games since their inception--ancient Games included--and so, despite some popular claims to the contrary, no one event or nation placed a permanent political stain on a previously unblemished Olympics.

Armed with this background, readers can best understand the detailed analysis of the politics of the Los Angeles Games presented in Chapter Three. The investigation probes not only the who and the what of 1984 Olympic politics but the how and the why as well.

Chapter Four focuses on the future of the Olympic Games. The conclusion discusses the aftermath of the 1984 Los Angeles Games, previews the 1988 Seoul Games, and evaluates proposals for Olympic reform using the evidence found in the first three chapters.

If there is one moral in this exposition, it is that idealism needs to be distinguished from realism. While idealism in itself is not harmful, the failure to acknowledge reality and its constraints can be damaging. Olympic mythology--as exemplified by Zola Budd--proves this point as well as any fable.

My interest in politics and the Olympics, particularly with respect to the Los Angeles Games, stems largely from my dual experience reporting on the 1984 Olympics and working--in a very minor capacity--on the press staff of the Los Angeles Olympic Organizing Committee (LAOOC). But interest alone did not make this work a reality. Significant research material came from the wondrous library collections of the University of California, Berkeley. Much of the information about the 1984 Games was culled from the *Los Angeles Times*, and kudos are due to the newspaper and particularly to Kenneth Reich, who covered the Los Angeles Games from the city's 1977 bid and on through a decade. My acknowledgment and appreciation for assistance go to Bill Davis and Greg Coan. Finally, my thanks go to Kathleen Moran, Mom, and Dad, for putting up with my seemingly endless shenanigans. At last, they have ended.

Epigram: Zola Budd, as quoted in *Los Angeles Times*, January 28, 1984.

SPORT AND POLITICS

Chapter One
A PRIMER ON SPORT AND POLITICS

I really don't think politics and sports should be mixed at all.
              John Gregorek, Olympic steeplechase athlete

Moscow just called and they think Marcus Allen is our secret weapon and they insist we dismantle him. If you turn him over to us, we'll put him in our silos and we wouldn't have to build and deploy MX missiles.
              U.S. President Ronald Reagan to coach Tom Flores after Allen led Flores's team to the Super Bowl championship

The Eastern bloc boycott of the 1984 Los Angeles Olympic Games evoked cries similar to John Gregorek's from athletes around the world. If those cries sounded familiar, it is only because they were echoes of the chorus of pleas heard in 1980, when the West boycotted the Moscow Olympics.

The theme of these athletes' cries is that sport should be above politics. Implicit in that belief is the conviction that sport and politics are separable spheres of culture. Olympic ideals reflect this conviction, and so do many people touched by the Olympic Games--not only athletes but administrators, judges, journalists, and fans as well.

A simple definition of ideal is "not real," and the ideal that sport and politics should--indeed, can--be separate clearly fits that definition. Keeping politics out of the Los Angeles Games was as much an ideal as keeping pollution out, and anyone who believed either ideal could become real could best be described as engaging in wishful thinking. The politics of the 1984 Olympics are most clearly understood within the context of the relationships between sport and society, both in the United States and throughout the world.

"Sports are games played by children and vivacious grown-ups," says James Michener. "They serve us best when they are restricted to their proper sphere."[1] Michener's thought is noble, but he confuses sport with play. The latter represents the generally spontaneous--or at least unsupervised--activity of "children and vivacious grown-ups." Images of play include classmates playing tag on the school playground or neighborhood youth enjoying a game of stickball in the street. That game of stickball--children at play--becomes sport in a format like Little League. Among the differences: in stickball children make up the rules as needed, in Little League the rules are codified and children have no say in their development or application; in stickball the game ends when the players want it to end, in Little League the game ends when the rules say it ends; in stickball the children themselves run the game, in Little League everyone but the children run the game, from team coaches through national officials.

Sport takes play and institutionalizes it through what Harry Edwards calls the three R's: rules, roles, and relationships.[2] Jay Coakley lists several characteristics that form an important but not exhaustive list of criteria that are met as a game becomes institutionalized:

1. The rules of the activity are standardized.
2. Rule enforcement is taken over by official regulatory agencies.
3. The organizational and technical aspects of the activity become important.
4. The learning of game skills becomes formalized.[3]

Sport in general, then, is a social institution. So is education, and it is easy to imagine the institutionalization process as the catalyst in changing education from parents teaching their children in the home to multibillion-dollar school districts involving elected officials, administrators, counselors, nurses, psychiatrists, and buses. Standardization and administration are as important in the institutionalization of education as well as of sport.

Michener--and the idealistic athletes--desire that sport be "restricted to [its] proper sphere." A society, however, does not consist of separate institutional components. Rather, it is the interplay of institutions-- sport and education are two; religion, the military, and the media are three others--that makes up a society.

Because it is a social institution, sport cannot be autonomous from the rest of society. The following glimpses of the contemporary United States will illustrate sport's relationships with other institutions as well as its role in society as a whole.

> The amount of attention devoted to athletics would be striking to an innocent visitor to a high school. A visitor would likely be confronted, first of all, with a trophy case. His examination of the trophies would reveal a curious fact: the gold and silver cups, with rare exception, symbolize victory in athletic contests, not scholastic ones. The figures adorning these trophies represent men passing footballs, shooting basketballs, holding out batons; they are not replicas of "The Thinker." The concrete symbols of victory are old footballs, basketballs, and baseballs, not works of art or first editions of books won as literary prizes. Altogether, the trophy case would suggest to the innocent visitor that he was entering an athletic club, not an educational institution.[4]

> Newspapers devote an entire section of their daily editions to the coverage of sport. Newsprint about sport surpasses even that given to our economy, politics, or any other single topic of interest. Television brings into our homes over 1200 hours of live and taped sporting events every year, sometimes disrupting our family life and other times providing a collective focus for our family's attention. Sport personalities from over 100 major professional sport team franchises serve as objects of our attention and as our heroes and anti-heroes. Our children are more apt to be familiar with the names of Tony Dorsett and Tracy Austin than with those of Andrew Young and Sandra Day O'Connor.[5]

> It was during a Monday night NFL half-time show that I first became aware that football games had become a heady mix of patriotism, sex, violence, and religion. A bloody first half had barely ended when hordes of personnel flooded the field, carrying flags, and trumpets, and small cannon, and rifles, and Bibles. They were joined by eighty-six scantily clad girls in age groups ranging from fourteen years old to twenty-five. This

> was a combination of American values hard to
> beat, with marines and rabbis and priests
> adding sanction to the affair. It was
> difficult, at times, to tell whether I was in
> a strip-tease show, an armory, a cathedral,
> or a ball park.[6]

Sport affects--and is affected by--something as basic to society as language:

> Men may refer to a woman as a *knockout*. Many
> things come *out of left field*, people who
> can't *get to first base* sometimes *throw in
> the towel* and start from *scratch*, and
> virtually all of us at times feel *under par*
> or find ourselves *behind the eight ball*.[7]

Play, then, can be "restricted to [its] proper sphere"--that is, the lack of formal "rules, roles, and relationships" somewhat distances play from institutionalized, well-defined, established society. But sport, as we have used the term, is not only part of society but also one of a number of institutions whose interrelationships largely define a society.

The excerpts above emphasize that sport cannot be separate from education, the media, or any other sphere of society, because all of those spheres intersect. While one child's play might not affect U.S. culture, it is often claimed that sport builds the character and spirit of the nation.[8] Whether this is indeed true is open to debate, but the mere perception indicates sport's powerful role in U.S. society. Observers no less important than presidents have noted this relationship. "Next to religion," said Herbert Hoover, "baseball has furnished a greater impact on American life than any institution."[9] Gerald Ford adds, "Outside of a national character and an educated society, there are few things more important to a country's growth and well-being than competitive athletics."[10]

Harry Edwards, an organizer of the 1968 Olympic Project for Human Rights (OPHR), understood the relationship between sport and society perfectly. In describing the foundation of OPHR, a black athletes' protest movement centered on the 1968 Mexico City Olympics, Edwards said it was "our belief that the role of blacks in American sports was intimately interdependent with our overall struggle for human rights in American society."[11] Increasingly, today's sports pages are filled with stories not about games but about players' strikes, drugs, alcohol, million-dollar contracts, and ill-tempered athletes. While some Americans claim that this is not what sport is all about, Richard Mandell shrewdly observes, "These celebrated aberrations may instead illustrate the profundity of the integration of formal sport into American life."[12] If we note Mandell's careful use of the term "formal sport"--as opposed to play--we see that he eloquently makes the very point we have been stressing.

In establishing that sport is not separate from society but instead a critical component of society, we have to this point avoided mention of another critical component of society: politics. The term "politics" here has a dual meaning. We will primarily speak of the traditional notion of politics--that is, the governing process and its underlying ideological system. In this sense, politics is an institutional sphere of society that--like sport, education, or any other sphere--has its own rules, roles, and relationships. However, we also use the word "politics" in a subtle sense to categorize the processes and products of institutionalization. For example, the institutionalization of U.S. education is not neutral. United States society demands that the U.S. system of government, for instance, often serve as the only form studied in government classes. For good or bad, what is taught and who decides it are not neutral decisions, and the term "politics" can reasonably be applied here. Clearly, the second meaning of politics, as we use the term, is dependent on the first to provide the appropriate cultural contexts for discussion and comparison.

We have now established that sport and politics are two of the many institutional spheres whose interrelationships largely constitute a society. In fact, the links between sport and politics are so prominent and numerous that even the devoted idealist who wishes that the two spheres be separate should be able to see in the following evidence a distinction between idealism and realism.

Ronald Reagan's quote at the opening of this chapter is a paradigm of the relationship between sport and politics. Well aware that the Super Bowl attracts many more viewers than any presidential address or news conference,[13] Reagan lent a political air to the game merely by appearing on national television to congratulate the winning team. But Reagan went farther, turning his appearance into a partisan political forum by using the name of the game's most valuable player in connection with a hotly debated weapons system that the president was trying to push through Congress. In 1985, the next year, Reagan let the Super Bowl take precedence over his second inauguration on its constitutionally mandated day, January 20. He kept his ceremony small and allotted time to appear before a national television audience during the game broadcast-- twice.

Reagan is not the first president to associate himself with the sporting world. Richard Nixon started the trend of presidents calling to congratulate championship coaches and once even suggested a play to George Allen, the coach of football's Washington Redskins.[14] In fact, the custom of presidents appearing at sporting events goes back at least to 1910, when William Howard Taft threw out the ceremonial first pitch at a baseball game.[15] Even before then--five years before, to be precise--Theodore Roosevelt called football officials to the White House and ordered them to clean up what was then an intensely violent and dangerous game.[16] Back in 1905, then, sport was regarded as an integral part of society and as an institution interrelated with politics.

It is not only the executive branch of politics that mixes with sport. Congress has granted baseball an exemption to federal antitrust law, has legislated rules governing football on television, and is now considering several bills to regulate city-to-city moves of professional sports franchises. Local government is involved, too, in the sensitive areas of public financing of sports stadia and keeping or attracting professional athletic teams.[17] Perhaps the move of the Oakland Raiders football team to Los Angeles is the best example of sport and politics and their place in society. The National Football League (NFL) challenged the move in court and lobbied congressmen to introduce and support the regulatory legislation alluded to above. Even more profoundly, the city of Oakland challenged the move on the basis of eminent domain, a legal power granted to cities to condemn something--usually land--needed for local use, typically roads or buildings but never an athletic team.[18] Both the NFL and Oakland eventually lost lengthy and costly court cases. A doubter of the links between sport and politics might be swayed by this evaluation of the 1983 Raiders season. "Our team battled not only opponents on the field," said team executive Al LoCasale, "but a powerful combination of the NFL's propaganda machine, the federal courts, the state courts, the halls of Congress."[19]

The relationships between sport and politics are evident in American speech:

> Politicians play *hardball*. Even presidents have *game plans* and win elections in *photo finishes*. Issues often become *political footballs*. Men with power are *heavyweights* and have *clout*. Labor negotiators throw out *ballpark figures*. *Kickoff* dinners start all kinds of campaigns.[20]

Perhaps the best recent example of sport jargon finding its way into politics comes during elections. Not only have the media taken to calling elections "horse races," but coverage of elections--most notably the long presidential campaign--has begun to resemble coverage of

actual horse races. The media concentrate on who won, who
lost, and by how much, with numbers, figures, and
statistics replacing substantive information on either
horses or candidates.[21]

Politics and sport intersect in U.S. society in ways
not particular to a specific politician. The values
stressed in U.S. society are reflected in both politics and
sport. Competition is a prime example, as Vice President
Spiro Agnew pointed out:

> Football as we know it is a uniquely American
> game, emphasizing some of the finest aspects
> of our national character. We are a
> competitive people, and it is the spirit of
> competition which has made our economic
> system the envy of the world. It's the
> competitive spirit among the young that
> causes excellence in adult life.[22]

Agnew's cause and effect can be debated, but his focus
on competition cannot be. Whatever the institutional
sphere, Americans speak of winning and of being number one.
We noted earlier the trend of presidents congratulating
winning teams in championship games. No such accolades are
ever in order for the losing teams, even if that team is
the second best out of several dozen--no small
accomplishment in itself, but not number one. Political
"races" involve "running for office," and U.S. government
operates on a "winner take all" system, most notably in the
processes of selecting congressmen and presidents, to an
extent unheard of in any other political system. In
business, Mandell observes, "Executives inspire their
underlings by emphasizing the 'team,' 'team playing,'
'winning,' establishing sales 'records,' being 'number
one,' 'rankings' with competitors and other teams."[23] The
competitive nature of U.S. society is reflected not just in
and by sport but in and by politics and other institutional
spheres as well.

Another and more subtle aspect of competition in
American society involves the economic system under which
the United States operates. That system is capitalism, and
its invisible hand reaches out of the economic sphere and
into the realms of politics and sport. Although U.S.
politicians and their advisers--economists--do not always
agree on how a capitalist economy should be managed, policy
makers and planners throughout the mainstream ideological
system--Edward Kennedy to Ronald Reagan and John Kenneth
Galbraith to Milton Friedman--agree on the general
principle of capitalism. Inherent in a capitalist system is
the spirit of free enterprise. It is therefore no surprise
to find that entrepreneurs are responsible for much of the
development of U.S. sport--laissez-faire politics is still

politics--with profit or loss serving as the ultimate definition of winning. In fact, the chance for increased profit is often cited as one of Branch Rickey's motives in making Jackie Robinson the first modern (post-1900) black major league baseball player.[24]

U.S. attitudes toward gender and race relations weigh heavily in the nation's social institutions. Until very recently, prominent female and black athletes were no more common--to be precise, no more uncommon--than female and black politicians. The same holds true for other spheres of society. As Mandell notes, "Enlightened or progressive views of social morality in America . . . conflicted with American tradition regarding the separation of the races"[25] and genders. As the United States changes, awareness of the interrelationships between sport and politics is evident in laws, such as the 1972 Title IX statute banning sex discrimination in education and paving the way for women's high school and college athletic programs, and movements, such as Harry Edwards's OPHR.

Presidential campaigns and declarations, court cases, free enterprise, gender and race relations, and capitalism are not topics one readily associates with sport. What the preceding pages have attempted to demonstrate is that sport and politics, as institutional spheres, are interdependent with--not independent of--each other and U.S. society as a whole. What the preceding pages have not attempted to determine is whether this mixing of sport and politics is good or bad. In order to understand the political aspects of the Olympic Games, one needs to recognize the inherent political nature of sport. Beyond that recognition, the relationships between sport and politics can be regarded as good or bad, but those relationships cannot be naively wished away--as John Gregorek does at the opening of this chapter--if they are to be studied.

This introduction to sport and politics has focused on the United States for two reasons. First, the reader is likely to be most familiar with sport, politics, and society in the U.S. context. More important, though, the strong connections that exist between sport and politics in the United States are, for all their webs, among the weakest in the world. The primary reason for this irony is that the U.S. government is one of the few whose politics-- in ideology as well as in practice--do not provide for nationwide federal involvement in sport. National athletic plans and a ministry of sport exist in most other countries.

"Richard Nixon was a particularly intense sports fan. As a strong leader he attempted fundamental government changes that were almost coups d'etat," observes Mandell. "However, Nixon never considered instituting any sort of national sports policy."[26] As we have seen, sport and politics still blend in the United States. It stands to reason, then, that this blend would be even smoother in countries with direct government involvement in sport. Several glances around the globe will validate this hypothesis.

Our brief world tour begins in China. Li Menghua is the minister in charge of the State Commission of Physical Culture and Sports. The existence of this commission is evidence in itself of the official ties between sport and politics that do not exist in the United States. Li is frank about the political nature of his commission's mission. "The purpose in developing physical culture and sports in China," says Li, "is to popularize sports among the people, enhance their physique, improve the sports skills of the country as a whole and chalk up new records, and thus *help to promote the country's economic as well as ethical and cultural development*."[27] Li is equally forthright about the link between sport and politics under the current socialist system. "China's sports have undergone several thousand years of development," he says. "But they had not been regarded as an undertaking of the state until 1949, when the People's Republic of China was founded."[28]

In contrast with the entrepreneurs, free enterprise, and individual competition of U.S. society in general, and sport and politics in particular, stand socialist societies. Sport--like business--is financed by government, not by the (nonexistent) private sector, and socialist governments establish socialist sport. Uses for sport in these societies include the promotion of team cooperation and collectivism, both of which dominate institutional spheres outside sport.

"Sport in . . . the Soviet Union is a serious business, with serious functions to perform," comments James Riordan. "It is associated with health, hygiene, defense, patriotism, integration, productivity, international recognition, even nation-building."[29] As Figure 1 shows, the Soviet government significantly regulates the means toward those ends. Such a wide range of goals encourages emphasis on popular participation. In socialist nations, sport involvement is maximized through youth training, on-the-job exercise and off-the-job sporting activity, and sport academies. Note in the Chinese example the interdependency of sport and politics with another sphere of society, the media, and the role of government in all: "The State Council stipulates that factory workers and government employees take a ten minute break to do setting up exercises both in the morning and in the afternoon. During these intervals, both the central and local radio stations broadcast special music for these exercises."[30] In the Soviet Union, students at the Central

FIGURE 1

Reprinted from James Riordan, *Soviet Sport*, Oxford: Basil
Blackwell, 1980. Reprinted with permission of Basil
Blackwell Publishers and Washington Mews Books, a division
of New York University Press.

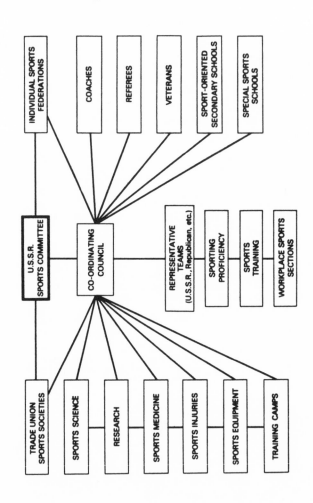

Institute of Physical Culture--the nation's would-be coaches--discuss not only sport techniques and education but also Communist Party history, Marxist-Leninist philosophy, and working conditions of factory laborers and farmers.[31] In China, the government approves which sports may be officially played.[32]

Nicaragua provides a fresh look at sport and politics. The national pastime, as in the United States, is baseball. But the ruling Sandinistas recently placed their stamp on the game. The government subsidizes all ten major league teams, helping to cover operating expenses and a pension plan for players. In return, the players march in revolutionary celebrations. The national stadium is named after Rigoberto Lopez Perez, who killed the founder of the Somoza family dynasty, the rulers of Nicaragua before the Sandinistas took power. Most clearly in line with the spirit of collectivism is a new edict that limits the number of innings a pitcher can throw each week, an effort to avoid injuries and lengthen careers and a slap at U.S. notions of competition.[33] Ottoniel Arguello, the president of the Nicaraguan Baseball Federation, explains, "We do not want the players to be used merely as objects of investment and spectacle. We want a more humane system that takes into account the player's education, health, and family and gives him a chance to develop as a person."[34]

Whether the politics in sport involves the capitalism that Arguello despises or the socialism that he advocates, this chapter has attempted to illuminate the links among sport, politics, and society. In the United States, where we have seen a pronounced interdependence among institutional spheres, the bonds are perhaps the weakest of any major nation because of the lack of direct government involvement in sport. Where such involvement exists, the already deep relationships between sport and politics become even deeper. The mixing of sport and politics may be regarded as good or bad, but it is a fact that needs to be recognized in order to comprehend the political nature of the Olympics.[35]

In a moment, we will turn our attention to the Olympic Games, but let us present a final piece of evidence, a 1966 editorial from a British newspaper, to show that sport is not isolated from society or any of its institutional spheres. A line from a discussion of the following day's World Cup soccer championship game between England and Germany will serve as the last word here. "If perchance on the morrow Germany should beat us at our national game," read the editorial, "let us take consolation from the fact that twice we have beaten them at theirs."[36]

NOTES

Epigram 1: John Gregorek, as quoted on *Nightline, May 8, 1984*.

Epigram 2: Ronald Reagan, as quoted in *Los Angeles Times*, January 23, 1984. The Super Bowl is. the championship game of professional football in the United States.

1. Michener, p. 378.
2. Edwards (1983), lecture.
3. Coakley, pp. 7-10.
4. Coleman, p. 441. He continues: "Walking further, the visitor would encounter teen-agers bursting from classrooms. Listening to their conversations, he would hear both casual and serious discussions of the Friday football game, confirming his initial impression. Attending a school assembly that morning, he would probably find a large segment of the program devoted to a practice of school yells for the athletic game and the announcement of a pep rally before the game. At lunch hour, he would be more likely to find more boys shooting baskets in the gymnasium than reading in the library. Browsing through a school yearbook, he would be impressed, in his innocence, with the number of pages devoted to athletics. Altogether, this visitor would find wherever he turned a great deal of attention devoted to athletics."
5. Coakley, p. 2.
6. Michener, p. 383.
7. *Los Angeles Times*, March 17, 1985. Quoting further from that article: "Many football writers today tell us of *battles that are won in the trenches*, teams that use *nickel defenses* and *flea-flickers* and quarterbacks who avoid *blitzes* to *throw bombs* or *dying quails*, *eat the ball to kill the clock* or *audibilize* when somebody *shoots the gap*.

"Baseball writers talk of *nubbers*, *insurance runs*, *comebackers*, *scroogies*, *bleeders*, and *bloopers*, and of pitchers who throw *flame*, *aspirin tablets*, *fog*, and *smoke*. Close plays are *bang-bang*, and *choppers* that are hit off *breaking balls* are sometimes turned into *broken-bat singles* on the carpet. Outfielders make *circus catches* and have *cannons* or *rifles* for arms. Batters who *hit with power* can drive the ball into the next ZIP code." (emphasis in original)
8. For views on whether sport actually does build character and national spirit, see Michener, pp. 12-17, and Coakley, pp. 16-55.
9. Quoted in Coakley, p. 17.
10. Quoted in Coakley, p. 33.
11. Edwards (1980), p. 175.
12. Mandell (1984), p. 232.
13. An estimated 110 million Americans--roughly half the nation's citizenry--watched Super Bowl XIX on Sunday,

January 20, 1985. "Far fewer Americans," wrote Howard Rosenberg, "saw [Reagan's] public inauguration . . . on Monday than saw him flip the coin to start Sunday's Super Bowl and afterward stiffly congratulate winning coach Bill Walsh." These events are referred to at the end of the present paragraph in the text. See *Los Angeles Times*, January 22 and 23, 1985.

14. For more on Nixon and sport, see Sage, pp. 7-8, and Michener, pp. 266-267, 378-381, and 420-423. See especially p. 380, where Michener says, "There was a calculated move in the Nixon administration to align sports and politics in such a way that nationalism became the end product." Adds Michener, "Nixon's own code name during the attack on Cambodia was 'The Quarterback.'"

15. Neft, p. 48.

16. See Michener, p. 87.

17. For more examples, see Michener, pp. 375-419.

18. *Newsweek*, July 26, 1982.

19. *Sports Illustrated*, September 5, 1984.

20. *Los Angeles Times*, March 17, 1985. (emphasis in original)

21. For specific comments on the now common "horse race" analogy, see Greenfield, pp. 26 and 273. For more general comments on media coverage of elections, see Greenfield, chapters 1 and 15.

22. Quoted in Michener, p. 100.

23. Mandell (1984), p. 274.

24. See Mandell (1984), pp. 182 and 274.

25. Mandell (1984), p. 223.

26. Ibid., p. 275.

27. Press Commission of the COC (1984b), pp. 2-3. (emphasis added)

28. Ibid., p. 2.

29. Riordan, p. 3.

30. Press Commission of the COC (1984b), p. 63.

31. Riordan, p. 166-167.

32. Press Commission of the COC (1984b), p. 5.

33. *San Francisco Chronicle*, March 18, 1985.

34. Ibid.

35. For comments and analysis on sport and society in detail and beyond the scope of this work, see Michener and also Edwards (1973), particularly the chapter on the American Sports Creed.

36. Quoted in Michener, p. 427.

Chapter Two
POLITICS AND THE OLYMPICS

*The Olympiads have been re-established for
the rare and solemn glorification of the
individual athlete.*
> Baron Pierre de Coubertin, founder
> of the modern Olympic Games

*[The Olympic Games] are really a political
instrument now more than anything else.
Athletes are totally disregarded in the
equation.*
> Robert Jiobu, sociologist

The city is Berlin, the year is 1936, the scene is the
Games of the XI Olympiad. The event is the long jump, and
the competitor is Jesse Owens. Since Owens holds the world
record of 26 feet, 8-1/4 inches, leaping the 23 feet, 5-1/2
inches needed to qualify for the finals should be a mere
formality for him.

Each athlete gets three attempts to jump the
qualifying distance. But Owens, tired from running in the
200-meter dash, fouls on his first two tries. If he does
not reach the 23-foot, 5-1/2-inch standard on his last
leap, the Olympic long jump finals will not include the
world's best long jumper.

While Owens prepares for his final attempt, a rival
jumper named Luz Long taps him on the shoulder. Long
suggests that Owens begin his jump several inches behind
the takeoff board. He could thus eliminate any chance of
fouling and, with his ability, still leap far enough to
meet the qualifying standard.

Owens realizes that Long is correct and makes the

adjustment--and, then, the final long jump competition. In that contest, Owens wins the gold medal on his last jump, narrowly defeating the altruistic Long, who captures the silver medal. The two athletes celebrate their performances--both of which surpassed the previous Olympic record--together.[1]

This tale is one of the most enduring in Olympic lore. Long's noble gesture--aiding the athlete who would later defeat him for the gold medal--certainly deserves to be remembered as a fine example of sportsmanship. Coubertin's Olympic ideal, that the important thing is not winning but taking part, could have no better exemplar than Long.

As touching as this story is, there are numerous other instances of athletes personifying Olympic ideals. This particular tale endures primarily because of its political overtones. When the International Olympic Committee (IOC) awarded the 1936 Games to Germany--then under the Weimar Republic government--in 1932, the Nazis, then a minority political party, opposed the award. An international festival that celebrated the achievement and effort of all mankind was incompatible with Nazi ideology that proclaimed the existence of a "master race." However, after the Nazis took power in 1933, Propaganda Minister Joseph Goebbels persuaded Adolf Hitler that the Games offered an exceptional opportunity to consolidate power at home and showcase Nazism abroad.[2]

Luz Long represented the epitome of Hitler's master race. Tall, blond, and muscular, he was the prototypical Aryan that Hitler wanted so desperately to propagate. Jesse Owens, on the other hand, was black--a synonym for "inferior" insofar as Nazi ideology was concerned. Long's assistance to Owens surely infuriated Hitler, and Long's defeat pained Hitler. As Owens said of his German rival, "It took a lot of courage for him to befriend me in front of Hitler."[3] The political setting of this story accounts for much of its continuing popularity.

Chapter One provided an introduction to sport and politics at the domestic level. The connections between these two societal spheres are no less pronounced on the international level. The cultural exchanges so popular in diplomacy involve sports teams as well as ballet companies and scientists, and the purposes are the same whether the performances take place in a stadium, an auditorium, or a laboratory. Fostering such exchanges can help maintain cordial relations between countries or help improve poor relations, as happened when a U.S. table tennis team visited China in 1971, paving the path toward the eventual establishment of normal diplomatic ties between the two nations.[4] Conversely, spurning such exchanges generally reflects an acrimonious atmosphere. The Supreme Council for

Sport in Africa, for instance, was founded by a South African anti-apartheid leader with the goal of ostracizing South Africa from international sport because of its discriminatory racial policies.[5] David Kanin calls sport a "risk-free"[6] tool in foreign affairs. "Sporting activities are simply not as vital," notes Kanin, "as economic, legal, or diplomatic relations."[7]

If politics colors sport within nations, it might reasonably be expected to be similarly useful--and I use the term in both a positive and a negative sense--in international relations. James Riordan provides the Soviet model:

> Soviet sport follows foreign policy and has important functions to discharge. These functions include winning support for the USSR and its policies among developing nations; maintaining and reinforcing the unity of the socialist countries; gaining recognition and prestige generally; and, most important of all, demonstrating the advantages of the Communist way of life. As a consequence, besides winning world championships and Olympic medals, talented Soviet athletes are expected to be ambassadors of good will and models of propriety in the arenas and forums of the world.[8]

The Russians, of course, are not the exclusive employers of sport in foreign policy. One can substitute "American" for "Soviet," "United States" for "USSR," "Western" for "socialist," and "capitalist" for "communist" in the above paragraph to obtain a clear U.S. view of international sport and international politics.

Let us focus, though, on the Olympic Games. Not only do the Games provide a microcosm of sport and politics on the global level, they are also the world's premier athletic festival. We will proceed first by example and then by analysis as we explore the politics of the Olympic Games. By the end of the chapter, the reader should be able to understand why George Will writes that the idea of removing politics from the Olympics is "akin to removing pasta from fettuccine."[9]

The ancient Olympic Games, which took place from 776 B.C. to A.D. 393,[10] occupy a special place in the hearts of modern sportsmen, who sometimes tend to speak of this forerunner of organized athletic competition in hushed and almost reverent tones. Indeed, the ancient Olympics represented the best of classical Greece. "We may sing of no greater contest than Olympia,"[11] wrote the poet Pindar. "The simple religious festival in which they had their beginning," observes Bill Henry, "developed into . . . a carnival of culture and athletic prowess with all the color and pageantry of those classic days."[12] It is not our purpose here to present a history of the ancient Games. Instead, we will look at selected aspects of those contests to show that the interplay of politics and Olympic sports existed in the ancient as well as the modern Games.[13]

One cannot dismiss the points that follow by arguing that the ancient Olympics were a domestic event while the modern Olympics are international. Although we view Greece today as a single nation, the Greece of the classical period parallels contemporary notions of an international structure. Classical Greece was composed of city-states; Athens is one example, Sparta another, and Elis--home of the ancient Olympic Games--a third. Each city-state was a sovereign entity, and the idea of a united Greek nation-state in those times was no more realistic than the concept of a federally powerful United States in the colonial era. The ancient Games, then, can be seen as a gathering of sovereign city-states, not just a national festival, and thus similar to the present Olympian assembly of nation-states. Many political issues surrounding the modern Games, in fact, have antecedents in classical times.

The most prominent of political decisions relating to the Olympics is whether to participate. The boycott is not a modern conception, however. Athens used the threat of nonparticipation in protesting a fine assessed against one of its athletes in the fourth century B.C.[14] Also, then as now, some states are not allowed to attend the Games. Sparta was barred from the Olympics of 420 B.C. for violating the sacred truce surrounding the Games.[15]

The city-states and athletes who did make it to the Olympics brought along political as well as sporting strategy. "There was," says M.I. Finley, "hardly a limit to the ways in which the passion for athletics and for victories could be capitalized on for ends that were in a broad sense political."[16] An Athenian ruler named Alcibiades demonstrated particular awareness of the political uses of the Games. In 416 B.C., after almost a decade of war with Sparta, Alcibiades entered seven chariots--an astounding number for a single city-state--to represent Athens, capturing first, second, and fourth places. The very entry of so many chariots told the Greek world that postwar Athens was far from weak and impoverished, and the success of those chariots fed Alcibiades's ego, domestic power, and political ambition.[17]

Political activity in the ancient Games was in many contexts dependent upon civic identification. Although each city-state did not select the equivalent of the contemporary national team, the Olympics were more than a contest of athletes competing solely for individual achievement and glory. Upon arriving at Olympia, participants registered their names and city-states.[18] After each event, heralds proclaimed the names of victors as well as their home city-states.[19] Winners received a crown of olive branches that generally ended up in the temple of the civic deity "as if it [the prize] belonged to the place which had produced the victor."[20] Although athletes did not officially represent their city-states, civic identification was readily apparent and ties between competitors and city-states emphasized. These elements comprise much of what we term "nationalism" in the modern Olympic Games.

Victory at Olympia brought prestige to city-states and their rulers, and political means to that success were not uncommon. After an athlete named Astylus won two events in the Olympic Games of 488 B.C., Gelon, the despot of Syracuse, induced him to switch his allegiance from his native Croton to Syracuse. Astylus competed as a Syracusan in the Games of 484 and 480 B.C., winning five events. This pleased Gelon but infuriated the citizens of Croton, who turned Astylus's house into a prison.[21]

Rewards for success were plentiful. The reception for Olympic victors coming home often outshone the return of a war hero. In 412 B.C., for instance, the triumphant Exainetos "entered [his city-state of] Akragas in a four-horse chariot, accompanied by three hundred of the most important citizens riding in chariots pulled by two white horses."[22] Olympic winners often became respected civic counselors and military figures.[23] Although the crown of olive branches was the only official Olympic award, "athletes expected and accepted material rewards for victory"[24] from their city-states. These rewards were primarily monetary; around 600 B.C., Athens showered any citizen who won at Olympia with a cash prize worth more than $300,000.[25] Tax exemption and free food for life were other common benefits.[26]

Today, of course, receipt of direct cash payments changes an athlete's status from amateur to professional and revokes Olympic eligibility. Contemporary Olympic officials continually err by claiming ancient athletes competed for no more than the love of sport. "The Greeks did not even have a word for 'amateur', only a word for 'athlete', meaning 'one who competes for a prize,'" remarks David Romano. "The idealistic image of an 'amateur,' which our modern athletes are told to emulate, did not exist in ancient Greece."[27]

It should be evident by now that politics pervaded the ancient Olympic Games in a variety of ways. David Kanin's conclusion provides a review and a preview. "The ancient Olympics were," says Kanin, "somewhat similar to the modern version in that political context was institutionalized in a system which allowed for the worship of the victor and the celebration of his homeland through his exploits."[28]

Before we examine the political elements intrinsic in the modern Olympic structure, let us discuss the Games as a sporting event. The Olympics are, at a fundamental level, an athletic festival. Some two dozen sports stage world championships at the Games, and officials of sports not presently represented in the Games continually clamor for inclusion on the Olympic slate. Despite the Soviet-led boycott, 7,800 athletes from 140 nations competed at Los Angeles in 1984.[29]

Even the United States, whose 597 participants comprised the largest national contingent at Los Angeles,[30] cannot boast of athletic proficiency or of national interest in every sport on the Olympic agenda. But every country involved enjoys enthusiasm for, if not talent in, several Olympic events. Indeed, an athletic federation must boast a membership of at least 50 countries before its sport can be included in the Games. Football--known to Americans as soccer--is immensely popular virtually everywhere outside the United States. Citizens of Eastern bloc nations follow weightlifting with the same passion that many Asians devote to field hockey, many Europeans to fencing, and many Americans to basketball. The combined quality and quantity of competition is unbeatable. One might well call the Olympic Games a buffet of sport, as there is truly something tasty for everyone.

The worldwide appeal of the Olympics provides the first clue in understanding their relationship to the political sphere. An event with global interest will receive global attention. If international sport and politics do mix--and our evidence indicates that they do-- then the preeminent international sporting event should have pronounced links with world politics. These ties will become evident in the following pages.

For the moment, one example serves to illustrate the significance of the Olympic Games in sporting as well as political terms. In 1979, several nations boycotted the world women's basketball championships, but the low visibility of the event obscured awareness of the boycott-- let alone awareness of the political motives and messages behind the boycott.[31] Of course, the influence of another societal sphere--the media--comes into play here. While women's basketball may not interest people around the globe, the diversity of Olympic sport as well as the Olympic spectacle itself mean worldwide attention from journalists as well as political figures--who can then use the assembled media for political purposes. In Los Angeles, more than 8,000 journalists received credentials to cover the Games--roughly one media member for each athlete involved.[32]

By any measure--including the number of athletes

competing, nations participating, or journalists reporting--the present scope of the Olympics is indeed imposing. One might reason that the widespread political activity in the Games implies that they are a victim of their own success. That is, the Olympic stage has been so effective in attracting a worldwide audience that political actors cannot resist the opportunity to share the stage with--and often steal the spotlight from--sports actors. This argument is only partially valid, for the Olympic Games have not only provided the stage but also joined the cast.[33] The politics of the Olympic movement are as important as any national or international political figures or events, and analyzing the former is essential to understanding the impact of the latter on what is superficially a purely athletic event.

Baron Pierre de Coubertin, the Frenchman credited with reviving the Olympic Games, envisioned them as much more than a sporting event. Coubertin, a young aristocrat, was disgusted by his homeland's poor showing in the Franco-Prussian War (1870-1871). He was convinced that the superior physical fitness of Germany's troops played a major part in France's military defeat, and he believed that his country's youth needed to sharpen their bodies as well as their minds. In addition, the baron thought that a worldwide athletic competition would be a significant contribution toward world peace and goodwill. National and international political interests thus colored Coubertin's decade-long struggle to stage a global sporting event.[34]

Coubertin used two societal models to help define his vague goal of an athletic festival. From ancient Greece, of course, the baron borrowed the name and concept of the Olympic Games. Coubertin, an idealist if nothing else, viewed the ancient Games in a utopian light, particularly with respect to the competitors:

> The young Greek passed the eve of contest in the solitude of the marble porticos of the gymnasium, far from the noise. He also had to be irreproachable personally and by heredity, without blemish either in his own life or that of his ancestors. He associated his act with the national religion, consecrating himself before an altar and receiving as token of victory a simple wreath, the symbol of genuine disinterestedness.[35]

Coubertin painted the picture of truly amateur athletes, devoted in their training and competing for the love of sport and for physical and mental development but not for any material inducements. From our earlier discussion, we can see that this picture is idealistic but incorrect. Nevertheless, Coubertin felt that the revived Olympic Games could fulfill his goal of generating goodwill among participants and their countries only if society did not "transform the Olympic athlete into the paid gladiator."[36] He was well aware that the classical Games ended-- concluding a remarkable durability of 1,000 years--only on the orders of the Romans who had invaded Greece.[37] Coubertin truly believed that following the Greek ideal--to be accurate, the Greek myth--of the true amateur was crucial in making the revived Olympics "a potent if indirect factor in securing universal peace."[38]

If Greece provided the name and ideals of Coubertin's movement, it was England that provided a relevant model. Although the baron could invoke the memories of classical Greece 1,500 years after the ancient Games ended, chariot races were not a part of nineteenth century sport. Coubertin, a confirmed Anglophile, found in England schools that emphasized development of body as well as mind, and he believed that physical education was a key to Britain's controlling an empire despite being far smaller than France. He proposed that France's schools adopt the English policy of instruction in physical and mental skills. France's athletic development could then be measured in competition with other countries, as Coubertin made English sport the foundation of the modern Olympics. British games were to be played at the Olympic Games.[39]

An unabashed admirer of Coubertin's idealism, John Lucas, comments that the baron's "life-long devotion to the Hellenic [Greek] trinity of body, mind, and spirit, coupled with a compelling faith in the character-building qualities of English sports education, formed the rationale for his dream of international amateur athletics."[40] Selling that dream to the world was another matter. In trying to use sport as a means to international harmony, Coubertin wisely realized that standardization of games and rules would provide a useful basis for intercultural interaction. As noted above, Coubertin selected British sport as the model for the world and the Olympics. While his idea of a unified athletic world did not encounter much opposition, his plan to use English sport as the catalyst did. Belgium and, ironically, Coubertin's native France resented the implication that their cultures were inferior to Britain's.

Even before the modern Olympic Games started, then, nationalism found its place in their political affairs. Nationalism also became part of their official political structure.[41] By and large, Coubertin did not try to sell his idea of an international athletic festival to the athletes. The sheer numbers of sportsmen would have made that a formidable task, to be sure, but Coubertin keenly concerned himself only with people in positions of power-- power to reform the French educational system in the English image, and power to turn the baron's Olympic dream into reality.

To accomplish the latter goal, Coubertin formed the International Athletic Congress. The baron invited government and national sporting association representatives to become delegates to the Congress, and the king of Belgium, the prince of Wales, and the crown prince of Sweden were among those accepting Congress membership.[42] Coubertin saw in his Olympic proposal an opportunity for international competition and, as a direct corollary, international goodwill. Most delegates at the Congress--representatives from state governments or state governing bodies of sports--saw the Olympics as an international competition and, as a direct corollary, a chance for "their" athletes to represent "their" nations and "their" systems against participants from other countries and other systems. International rivalry follows much more easily from this logic than does international goodwill.

Meeting in 1894, the Congress approved the concept of the Olympics and selected the first IOC, the quasi-legislative body that controls the Games. Committee members are not chosen by nations but by the IOC itself. Nevertheless, to this day, IOC members are associated with sovereign countries, not sporting associations or groups of athletes. The people running the Games were picked on the basis of their country, and so were the competitors. In this politically oriented structure, nationalism became inevitable.[43]

Ever the idealist, Coubertin campaigned long and hard--and often as a minority--against the inevitable. He cried out against such nationalistic trappings as medal counts, point scores, and the inclusion of team sports in the Games.[44] Coubertin apparently did not envision that politics would cloud his Olympic dream, despite helping to set up an essentially nationalistic organization to sponsor a competitive event. "Coubertin," Kanin pithily observes, "was abandoned by his movement."[45] In continuing to explain this estrangement, we will not give a chronological political history of the Olympic Games.[46] Instead, let us focus on assorted political themes throughout the annals of the modern Games.

Coubertin envisioned the Olympics as a festival of individual athletes from around the world. The Games, however, became a competition among national sports teams. The IOC members represent the IOC to their respective countries, taking away some measure of individualism. National Olympic committees (NOCs) represent their respective countries to the IOC, taking away any remaining hope for individualism. That is, the Games are not run by and for individuals per se, as Coubertin wished, but only by and for persons who happen to be affiliated with a nation.

In fact, the IOC has evolved to the point where it has

very little control over the operation of the Olympics--
which is what Coubertin logically thought would be its
primary function. The NOCs select national teams.
International federations--global governing bodies for
specific sports--run the athletic competition in their
particular sport. The organizing committee of the host
city, whether a private or state-sponsored group, controls
day-to-day management of the Games. Freedom from the burden
of actually staging the Games leaves the IOC much more open
to political matters.

The international assembly that is the IOC and the
international competition in the Games themselves provide a
dual world forum in which countries can express themselves.
Coubertin presented the ancient Olympics as a model for the
modern Games. As they developed, they indeed followed Greek
legacies in athletics--and politics. As noted earlier, the
most prominent political decision relating to the Olympics
is whether to participate. When the Soviet Union led a
boycott of the 1984 Los Angeles Games, many observers
blamed the United States for starting a boycott trend by
spurning the 1980 Moscow Games.[47] These commentators
ignored not only a significant boycott in 1976[48] but also a
political tradition dating back to ancient Greece.

The boycott--and its partner, the boycott threat--is a
political act in itself. The rationale behind such a stand
is generally political as well and often has little to do
with the Olympics. In fact, an Olympic boycott threat
predated the first modern Games. The French Gymnastics
Union declared that it would not attend the 1894
International Athletic Congress meeting if German
representatives were present. Despite Coubertin's talk of
international goodwill, some of his fellow Frenchmen did
not desire any kind of association with the Germans--
wartime enemies only 23 years before. The boycott never
materialized because Germany declined to send official
delegates to the Congress.[49]

After the Nazis took power in Germany, a vigorous
boycott movement swept the United States. A wide range of
groups believed that Hitler's anti-Semitic policies could
not be condoned through U.S. participation in the 1936
Berlin Games. Legendary sportswriter Damon Runyon wrote
that Nazi laws made Germany's living up to Olympic rules
"either an impossibility or a hypocrisy,"[50] and opposition
to sending a U.S. team to Berlin could be found in, among
other places, the American Jewish Congress,[51] the Catholic
magazine *Commonweal*, and the American Federation of
Labor.[52] In the end, the United States did participate in
1936. Avery Brundage, then president of the American
Olympic Committee,[53] convinced his cohorts that Germany's
promise to include Jews on its teams--a promise that was
honored--meant that Olympic guidelines were being followed.
Any further U.S. concerns regarding German policies and a

possible boycott, declared Brundage, would constitute the
unconscionable mixing of sport and politics.[54] Although the
United States did attend the 1936 Games, Ireland did not.[55]
It is unclear whether the Irish boycott was primarily meant
to protest German or British conduct.

Twenty years later, Brundage was president of the IOC.
Just before the 1956 Melbourne Games began, two world
crises erupted. In eastern Europe, Soviet tanks rolled into
Hungary and crushed a hint of a democratic rebellion.
Meanwhile, British, French, and Israeli forces advanced
into Egypt and seized the Suez Canal. Brundage, at times
even more captive to Coubertin's ideals than the baron
himself, commented on the Soviet invasion:

> Every civilized person recoils in horror at
> the savage slaughter in Hungary, but that is
> no reason for destroying the nucleus of
> international cooperation and goodwill we
> have in the Olympic movement. *The Olympic
> Games are contests between individuals and
> not between nations.*[56]

Six countries proved Brundage and his mythology incorrect.
The Netherlands, Spain, and Switzerland withdrew from the
Games to protest the Soviet action, while Egypt, Lebanon,
and Iraq boycotted over the Suez incident.[57] Ironically,
Hungary did participate, as its team had departed for
Melbourne before the invasion. In a graphic example of the
relationship between sport and politics, Hungary beat
Russia 4-0 in a violent and bloody water polo contest.
After the Games, 45 Hungarian athletes defected.[58]

Major boycott movements occurred in 1968 and 1976,
with South Africa the target on both occasions. Largely
because of that country's enthusiasm for and emphasis on
sport, black African nations have made international sport
a weapon in their battle to end apartheid, South Africa's
official policy of racial segregation and discrimination.
"The struggle to isolate South Africa in international
sport," Kanin comments, "has been the single most extensive
use of sport as an instrument of diplomatic and political
sanction."[59] This anti-apartheid campaign first manifested
itself in Olympic affairs in 1968. Four years earlier, the
IOC suspended South Africa for its NOC's failure to
guarantee that Olympic principles of equal opportunity
would be upheld. Given that apartheid was a national
policy, the South African NOC clearly could not make any
such guarantee.[60] Missing an Olympic Games chagrined that
sports-conscious country, which made token concessions--
including a mixed-race national team--in hopes of competing
in the 1968 Mexico City Games. These concessions pleased
Brundage, who viewed apartheid as an internal political
matter and therefore not an international sporting concern,

and the IOC restored membership to South Africa. Incensed black African nations declared they would boycott the 1968 Games, drawing support from the Soviet Union and some U.S. athletes. The IOC, after weighing the possible absence of 32 countries against the absence of South Africa alone, succumbed to political reality and again suspended South Africa.[61]

Even though the IOC expelled South Africa in 1970, its racial policies again became an issue in 1976. A New Zealand rugby team toured South Africa, prompting black Africa to again threaten an Olympic boycott, this time demanding the suspension of New Zealand. The rationale was curious, for, as Richard Espy points out, "New Zealand did not practice apartheid; rugby was not an Olympic sport; the New Zealand Rugby Federation was not affiliated with the New Zealand Olympic Committee; and the IOC had expelled . . . South Africa."[62] The puzzled IOC did not capitulate, and 30 nations did indeed boycott the 1976 Montreal Games, the first use of this venerable political weapon on such a large scale.[63] Black Africa's methods, though, were quite consistent with--and evidence of the seriousness of--its goal of isolating South Africa in the sporting world. "Sports and politics are these days body and soul," said Kenyan Foreign Minister James Osogo, demonstrating a much more realistic view of the world than the IOC. "We shall use all means available to us, including sports, to put pressure on South Africa until apartheid is wiped out."[64]

The Olympic movement sustained its largest boycott ever four years later. The United States led the way, as some 65 nations declined to participate in the 1980 Moscow Games, most doing so to protest the Soviet invasion of Afghanistan in December 1979.[65] Let us emphasize here, though, that a 1980 boycott was discussed well before the Russian military operation. In 1978, after the Soviets sentenced dissident Anatoly Shcharansky to 13 years in jail, his wife, Avital, traveled through western Europe and the United States, calling on Western nations to withdraw from the Moscow Games to protest Soviet treatment of dissidents and Jews.[66] Although Mrs. Shcharansky's momentum faded, the Russians revived it in January 1980 by sending another dissident, Andrei Sakharov, to internal exile. The Soviet Union had invaded Afghanistan only one month earlier, and U.S. anger continued to focus on that incident. Many countries, though, were more outraged by the Sakharov case. Russia's treatment of Sakharov played a significant role in the decisions of some nations to boycott, and more--including several key Western allies-- might have stayed away from Moscow had the United States emphasized Sakharov as well as Afghanistan in its boycott campaign.[67]

President Jimmy Carter chose Afghanistan as the reason the United States passed up the 1980 Games. Harry Edwards

reminds those idealistically descended from Coubertin and
Brundage that the president's "call for a boycott was a
political act, by a political person, in an arena second
only to the United Nations as an international political
forum."[68] Edwards, in fact, showed that sovereign nations
were not the only ones involved in the Olympics who could
play the boycott card--or threaten to. As an organizer of
the Olympic Project for Human Rights (OPHR), Edwards signed
up many star black U.S. athletes who pledged not to attend
the 1968 Mexico City Games. The OPHR did not protest any
international situation as much as it objected to U.S.
treatment of its black citizens.[69] The black athletes'
boycott did not materialize, but black American sprinters
Tommie Smith and John Carlos raised gloved fists on the
victory stand in a gesture of defiance and protest.
Although the IOC and the United States Olympic Committee
(USOC) ejected Smith and Carlos from the Olympic Village
and the U.S. team,[70] Kanin recognizes what the IOC and USOC
refuse to admit. "This non-violent demonstration," remarks
Kanin, "was as legitimate a use of political sport as any
by Olympic states."[71]

Nations hosting the Olympics certainly do not boycott
them, but they do employ their own strategies of political
manipulation. In the 1896 Athens Games, the Greek royal
family used these first of the modern Games to consolidate
and expand on its tenuous political power.[72] Germany's
Weimar Republic planned to use the 1936 Berlin Games to
showcase its revival from the ashes of World War I; the
world instead saw the Nazis' efficient spectacle.[73] The
organizers of the 1972 Munich Games went out of their way
to stage what Richard Mandell called "the anti-Nazi
Olympics," going so far as to avoid the color red because
of its Nazi association.[74] Japan managed to use the 1964
Tokyo Games to demonstrate its successful transition from
wartime loser to peacetime power.[75] The Soviet Union tried
to capitalize domestically and internationally on the 1980
Moscow Games, the first ever held in a socialist state.
Statements like this could be found in Communist Party
handbooks and official Russian Olympic information:

> The fact that Moscow has been entitled to
> stage the 1980 Olympic Games is the result of
> the purposeful, consistent, and peaceful
> foreign policy pursued by the Soviet Union, a
> bulwark of peace, democracy, and social
> progress, and the expression of the respect
> for the great Soviet achievements in physical
> education and sport.[76]

With such sentiments freely circulating around the Soviet
Union and the Eastern bloc, it is little wonder that Moscow
was acutely embarrassed by the widespread boycott of its

Games and infuriated by the preemption of its propaganda machine.[77]

All countries participating in the Olympic Games, not just the hosts, have the opportunity to use the Games for political purposes. In fact, individual nations need not conjure up elaborate schemes of political exploitation. Nationalistic elements--many of which are legacies of the ancient Games--abound in the Olympics. In addition to team selection on a national basis and the IOC's organization on a national basis, the Games themselves feature ample doses of nationalism. In the opening ceremony, participants march in national teams, wearing team uniforms and bearing the national flag. At each medal ceremony, each medalist's country is identified and its flag raised, and competitors stand at attention as the winner's national anthem is played.[78]

With each athlete competing not as an individual but for his or her country--indeed, wearing the country's name on his or her chest--identifying winners and losers is a simple task. Although Olympic rules forbid medal counts, they dominate Olympic media coverage as well as the propaganda of several successful states. For instance, the *New York Times* reported that the United States won the 1900 Paris Games.[79] The U.S. performed so well in the early Olympiads that it unsuccessfully petitioned the IOC in 1924 to officially recognize an Olympic point system that would have, in Kanin's words, "institutionalized American athletic superiority"[80] at the time. The United States was not alone in its claims of Olympic victory. Britain asserted that it had beaten the mighty Americans in the 1908 London Games,[81] and any number of German scoring systems showed the hosts victorious in the 1936 Berlin Games.[82] In 1952, both the United States and the Soviet Union boasted of winning the Helsinki Games. The U.S. point system emphasized gold medals, while the Russian scheme stressed all medals won.[83] One could not ask for a clearer reflection of sport in society. The U.S. point system, like America's capitalist society, emphasized competition and individual victory, while the Soviet point totals, like Russia's socialist society, stressed teamwork and cooperation.

Individual nations are not the only parties playing politics in the Olympics; the IOC also joins in the frolic. Although the IOC has no control over the actions of the NOCs, it does control which NOCs can join the Olympic family. Remembering that the N in NOC stands for "national," IOC recognition of a certain committee or acknowledgment of a certain name is tantamount to conferring diplomatic recognition for--given the Olympic media spectacle--all the world to see. IOC action in these cases generally reflects muddled idealism and eventual submission to global *realpolitik*. In 1948, for example, the

Palestine NOC had been accepted into the IOC, and the British territory planned to enter a team in the London Games. After the U.N. partition plan created the state of Israel, the Palestine NOC changed its name to the Israeli Olympic Committee and declared that its team would march behind the new Israeli flag in London. Arab nations, already upset over the U.N. action, believed those plans would imply Israeli legitimacy and threatened to boycott. The IOC reaction is less notable for its decision than for the bizarre logic behind it.[84]

> The IOC . . . solved the immediate problem by declaring Israel ineligible because the Israel Olympic Committee had been given recognition under the national designation of Palestine. Since the Palestine committee no longer existed, and since Israel had not applied for recognition, it was declared ineligible.[85]

Israel applied to participate in the 1952 Helsinki Games and--with support from the United States and the Soviet Union--was admitted to the Olympic family.[86]

In addition to the Israeli situation, the aftermath of World War II left the IOC with the issue of Germany. Unlike the Israeli situation, the German question was not resolved quickly and became greatly influenced by the Cold War. Postwar Germany had been split into two zones: the West, controlled by the United States, Britain, and France, and the East, occupied by the Soviet Union. The IOC--and, in general, the Olympics--have always had a Western orientation--founded by a Frenchman, modeled on English sports, and dominated by Americans, one of whom was in charge from 1952 to 1972. Avery Brundage's personal admiration for Germany and the mutual respect between that country and the Western-dominated IOC led to the 1951 recognition of the West German NOC as the sole Olympic representative of Germany.

At that time, both West and East German zones, like Brundage and the IOC, held some hope for eventual reunification. The IOC continued to consider Germany as one nation, and since IOC rules stated that only one NOC could represent each country, repeated requests for unconditional recognition of an East German NOC were denied for more than a decade. Brundage and the IOC instead worked for joint German teams, which--dominated by the larger West Germany-- did indeed appear in the Games of 1956, 1960, and 1964. Brundage boasted that these unified squads brought Germany together in a way politicians had been unable to do--the word "unwilling" would not have occurred to him--thus fulfilling Coubertin's dreams of international goodwill through sport. As Brundage told the IOC in 1963:

> Another example of an important victory for
> sport over politics has been the united
> German team . . . The spectacle of East and
> West German athletes in the same uniform
> marching behind the same leaders and the same
> flag is an inspiration under present
> political conditions.[87]

The word "illusion" would have been much more
appropriate than "inspiration." In 1955, East Germany
joined the Warsaw Pact, and West Germany and the Soviet
Union exchanged ambassadors. Six years later, the Berlin
Wall became a permanent symbol of the existence of two
distinct German nations. By 1962, the president of the West
German NOC called for an end to the "fiction" of the united
team, saying that separate West and East German teams were
"nothing else than the legislation of an existing state of
affairs."[88] Still, the IOC waited to recognize East
Germany's NOC--and thus acknowledge the existence of a
separate East Germany--until 1968, when numerous sports
federations and world governments had already done so. The
IOC's fancy of German reunification came to an ironic end
in 1972, when East Germany appeared in its first Games as a
nation with its own flag and anthem--in, of all places,
West Germany. The 1972 Munich Games showed East Germany's
sovereignty and athletic skill. They also showed, notes
Allen Guttmann, "the frailty of Olympic ideals and . . .
their inability to dam the tides of *realpolitik*.[89]

The game of diplomatic recognition is played by
individual countries, too. Olympic rules state that the
host country must allow within its borders for the duration
of the Games any national representative bearing an Olympic
identity card. In 1976, Taiwan entered the Montreal Games
as the Republic of China (ROC). Even though that name had
the IOC's sanction, Canada's one-China policy recognized
the People's Republic of China (PRC) as the sole legitimate
Chinese government. Admitting Taiwanese athletes under the
ROC name and banner would undermine foreign policy, the
Canadian government thought, and so it refused to allow the
Taiwan team to enter Canada unless the ROC name and flag
were dropped. Despite IOC efforts to reach a compromise,
both Canada and Taiwan felt that even partial capitulation
would weaken what each nation regarded as its legitimate
foreign policy, and Taiwanese athletes did not compete at
Montreal. Of course, the nationalistic structure of the IOC
and of the Games themselves made possible the Canadian
action.[90]

The U.S. reaction to this incident reveals much about
the relativistic nature of Olympic politics. Brundage's
homeland shared much of the IOC president's Olympic
idealism, and the United States condemned the African

nations that boycotted the 1976 Montreal Games for
improperly injecting politics into sport. Yet, since the
United States did recognize the Taiwanese government,
Canada's action prompted many U.S. leaders to call for an
American boycott of Montreal. The boycott weapon, then, was
not so revolting when brandished by the Americans, who not
only participated in but sparked a much larger boycott four
years later.[91] In addition, the Soviet Union turned
Canada's stand into Russian political prestige points by
assuring the IOC that all Olympians--even those from
Israel--would be admitted to the USSR for the 1980 Moscow
Games.[92]

The interplay between politics and the Olympic Games
has ben present in ancient and modern eras, but the
entrance of the Soviet Union into the Games, starting in
1952, has strongly nurtured that relationship. As long as
the modern Games remained in the domain of the Western
nations that shaped the revived Olympics in their own
image, ideological conflict in the Olympic context would be
minimal. As we have seen, the compatible ideologies of
charter IOC members did not keep them from fomenting
political activity in the Games. But such activity was
accentuated with the admission of the Soviet Union, whose
radically different ideology included numerous political
uses for sport. Riordan summarizes these applications on
page 17, but the point fundamental to all these uses is
that Russia did not share the Western--and Coubertinian--
view of sport as apolitical. The Soviet Union exploited the
nationalistic structure and global media coverage of the
Olympics--a Western-oriented festival, after all--to use
the success of its athletes as a metaphor for the success
of its political, economic, and social systems. Not
surprisingly, Western nations have responded to the Russian
challenge by following the Russian example. So, too, have
Soviet allies and Third World nations.[93]

Perhaps the greatest impact of the socialist approach
to sport has been in turning one strongly held Olympic
ideal into little more than a joke. That ideal is
amateurism, and it was invoked religiously by Coubertin and
Brundage.[94] Coubertin was an aristocrat, and most
competitors in the first several Olympics belonged to that
same social stratum. Very few citizens not in the upper
classes could spare time for sport. With most competing
nations having similar social--that is, Western--systems,
and hence similar definitions of amateurism, problems of
professional athletes were limited in scope as well as in
political nature. Thus, when Olympic officials stripped Jim
Thorpe of the decathlon and pentathlon gold medals he had
won in the 1912 Stockholm Games because he had accepted a
small sum of money to play baseball, the reaction was
restrained. The cries of injustice to Thorpe often heard
today were not nearly so loud at the time.[95]

In Western nations, professional sport leagues--for example, the NFL in the United States--allow a marked distinction between amateur and professional athletes. No professional alternatives--and therefore no such dichotomy--exist in socialist systems. Activity is directed toward the good of the state rather than the good of the individual. Athletes in socialist societies serve their countries in explicitly political ways and, hence, receive privileged treatment. This "state amateur," however, does not fit well into the Olympic scheme, which views an amateur athlete as one who devotes his energies to other endeavors outside the world of sport. The unquestioned success of athletes representing socialist countries has perplexed the IOC. These participants do meet the amateur standard that Thorpe did not, but that criterion is utterly inapplicable to state amateurs. While the IOC struggles to find a definition of amateurism relevant to the late twentieth century, both socialist and capitalist camps have used the stark contrast in their respective societal methods of training competitors as a basis for, on the occasion of victory, trumpeting oft-repeated claims that athletic success implies cultural superiority. The issues of amateurism and professionalism breed political controversy in the Olympic Games that goes far beyond payments to any particular athlete.[96]

Olympic politics would not be possible without Olympic athletes. The marvelous sporting performances by so many outstanding competitors should not be forgotten. They often are, though, as the Games possess a distinguished political legacy as well as a distinguished athletic legacy. The 1972 Munich Games, for example, are best remembered for the massacre of 11 Israeli Olympians by Arab terrorists, not for the seven gold medals won by swimmer Mark Spitz. In this chapter, the themes of nationalism, boycotts, and professionalism have been featured in illustrating the relationship between politics and the Olympic Games, a relationship dating back to ancient Greece. We have seen how Olympic ideals and lore represent more of mythology than of reality, and how that mythology helped create a modern Olympic structure built on politics and an inviting forum for political expression. Now, after looking at political themes from various Olympiads, we will closely examine the 1984 Los Angeles Games as a case study of Olympic politics.

Before we do, a final case deserves mention. The nation of Guyana boycotted the 1972 Munich Games and the 1976 Montreal Games. One of its athletes, James Gilkes, was a world-class sprinter. Gilkes sat out the 1972 Games but, four years later, did not know how long he could stay at the top of the track world and desperately wanted to test his skills in the top international competition offered in the Olympics. He thus went to Montreal[97] and requested that the IOC allow him to compete as an individual, wearing the Olympic logo and marching behind the Olympic flag. The IOC chose to make a statement for and not against nationalism in the Games, denying Gilkes's petition by saying that only national representatives--that is, those chosen by an NOC--could participate. Instead of taking a small step toward the festival of individuals that Coubertin envisioned, the IOC continued to ensure that the Olympics would remain a festival of nations. No action could be more telling in explaining the selection of quotes that appear at the opening of this chapter.[98]

NOTES

Epigram 1: Baron Pierre de Coubertin, as quoted in Henry, p. 8.

Epigram 2: Robert Jiobu, as quoted in *Sports Illustrated*, May 21, 1984.

1. Schaap, pp. 211-212, and Mandell (1971), pp. 166-167.

2. See Mandell (1984), pp. 237-245, and Kanin, pp. 52-53.

3. Quoted in Schaap, p. 212.

4. Espy, pp. 3-4.

5. Kanin, p. 100. "The issue of sport was just a vehicle for expressing Africa's general opposition to the South African policy of apartheid and white rule," notes Richard Espy. But "South Africa's intense preoccupation with sport provided an ideal arena of opposition for Africa's overall campaign." (Espy, p. 128)

6. Kanin, p. 1.

7. Kanin, p. 2.

8. Riordan, p. 52.

9. *Los Angeles Times*, May 10, 1984.

10. These dates, of course, can be no more than informed estimates. These estimates appear in Douskou and in Finley and Pleket.

11. Quoted in Douskou, p. 77.

12. Henry, p. 10.

13. Interested readers can find comprehensive accounts of the ancient Olympic Games in Douskou and in Finley and Pleket. Douskou is encyclopedic in scope and sympathetic in tone, while Finley and Pleket is more scholarly.

14. *Los Angeles Times*, July 22, 1984.

15. Douskou, p. 110.

16. Finley and Pleket, p. 100. As we will see, Finley might just as well be commenting on the modern Olympics.

17. Henry, p. 12; Kanin, p. 11; Finley and Pleket, p. 73.

18. Douskou, p. 110.

19. Douskou, p. 134.

20. Grenier, p. 31.
21. Finley and Pleket, p. 101.
22. Douskou, p. 136.
23. Douskou, p. 140.
24. Finley and Pleket, p. 71.
25. *Los Angeles Times*, August 2, 1984.
26. Douskou, p. 137.
27. *Los Angeles Times*, July 22, 1984.
28. Kanin, p. 11.
29. *Los Angeles Times*, July 28, 1984.
30. Ibid.
31. Leiper, pp. 105-106.
32. LAOOC (1984b), p. 5.
33. Espy calls the Olympic Games an "arena" in which the Olympic movement is a "participant."
34. See Guttmann, pp. 12-13, and Lucas, pp. 22-29.
35. Quoted in Henry, p. 21.
36. Quoted in Henry, p. 22.
37. See Henry, p. 21, and Douskou, pp. 282-285.
38. Quoted in Lucas, p. 29.
39. Lucas, pp. 22-30; Kanin, pp. 19-22; Mandell (1984), pp. 201-202.
40. Lucas, p. 23.
41. The uses of the word "politics" here intentionally reflect the two definitions of the word given in Chapter One. The IOC, as it evolves, will come to resemble a government by developing a "governing process and its underlying ideological system."
42. Henry, p. 23.
43. Kanin, pp. 19-23; Henry, pp. 19-24; Guttmann, pp. 12-15; Mandell (1984), pp. 201-203; Lucas, pp. 22-27.
44. Henry, p. 8. Medal counts and point scores are emphasized not only by nations, in trying to prove their athletes and systems superior, but by the media, in their quest for instant news and their perceived need to simplify matters to winners and losers.
45. Kanin, p. 22.
46. Kanin and Espy both provide comprehensive accounts of politics and the modern Olympic Games.
47. *Los Angeles Times*, June 2, 1984.
48. Espy, pp. 157-158. Thirty African nations boycotted the 1976 Montreal Games. See p. 26.
49. Henry, p. 23.
50. Quoted in Mandell (1971), p. 78.
51. Kanin, p. 53.
52. Mandell (1971), p. 77.
53. This body is now called the United States Olympic Committee (USOC).
54. Mandell (1971), pp. 69-82; Kanin, pp. 53-55; Guttmann, pp. 65-78; Schaap, pp. 213-214.
55. Kanin, p. 55.
56. Quoted in Guttmann, p. 162. (emphasis added)

57. Guttmann, pp. 161-163, and Espy, pp. 46-49, 53-55. Espy suggests that Spain and Egypt, because of financial difficulties, might not have sent teams to Melbourne anyway.

58. Guttmann, pp. 163-164, and Espy, pp. 54-55.

59. Kanin, p. 97.

60. Espy, pp. 85-87.

61. Espy, pp. 94-106. The Soviet Union has generally supported black Africa's efforts to exclude South Africa from international sport, primarily for the simplest of motives--trying to forge alliances with nonaligned Third World nations. This concern is of far more interest to the Soviets than are any human rights concerns.

62. Espy, p. 158.

63. Espy, pp. 157-158.

64. *Los Angeles Times*, July 18, 1976.

65. Kanin, pp. 116-117, 145.

66. *Los Angeles Times*, July 15, 1978; July 18, 1978.

67. Kanin, pp. 126-127.

68. *Los Angeles Times*, March 9, 1980.

69. Edwards (1980), p. 175. See also pp. 174-204.

70. Schaap, pp. 331-336.

71. Kanin, p. 94.

72. Kanin, p. 28.

73. Kanin, pp. 52-56, and Mandell (1984), pp. 241-245.

74. Mandell (1984), p. 255.

75. Espy, p. 76.

76. Quoted in Hazan, p. 84. See also *Los Angeles Times*, April 24, 1980.

77. *Los Angeles Times*, August 4, 1980.

78. Toohey and Warning, pp. 120-121, and Kanin, pp. 22-23, 27.

79. Kanin, p. 31.

80. Kanin, p. 48.

81. Kanin, p. 35.

82. Mandell (1971), p. ix.

83. Kanin, pp. 64-65.

84. Espy, p. 29.

85. Ibid.

86. Kanin, p. 103.

87. Quoted in Guttmann, p. 155.

88. Quoted in Espy, p. 79.

89. Guttmann, p. 157. More information on postwar Germany and the IOC can be found in Guttmann, pp. 150-157; Kanin, pp. 67-72; and Espy, pp. 42-43, 76-79, 106-108.

90. Espy, pp. 152-155, and Kanin, pp. 78-79.

91. Edwards (1984), pp. 41-43.

92. *Los Angeles Times*, August 3, 1976. The Soviets never got a chance to fulfill their promise; Israel boycotted the Moscow Games.

93. Edwards (1981), pp. 232-234.

94. In fact, Brundage's biographer calls him the

"apostle of amateurism." (Guttmann, p. 110)

95. Kanin, pp. 36-37, and Schaap, pp. 127-128. Thorpe eventually had his medals restored, posthumously and dozens of years after the fact.

96. Osterhoudt, pp. 42-44.

97. Gilkes lived in the United States and attended the University of Southern California, so for him to fly to Montreal was not as herculean a task as it would have been had he lived in Guyana.

98. *Los Angeles Times*, July 24 and 25, 1976, and Espy, p. 169.

Chapter Three
A CASE STUDY: POLITICS
AND THE LOS ANGELES GAMES

*The 1984 Olympics are the Games that nobody
wanted.*
> Harry Edwards, sociologist and
> Olympic activist

*These have been labeled the Olympics of
patriotism, of provincialism, of chauvinism,
of stinginess, of capitalism, of
exploitation, of U.S. isolationism, of
victory of professionals over amateurs, but
if I were to pass judgment on Los Angeles, I
would give it top marks as the best in
history.*
> One European's view of the
> 1984 Los Angeles Games

Whether the 1984 Los Angeles Games were the best ever
is open to question, and one's answer would no doubt depend
on one's criteria. But these Olympics, the Games of the
XXIII Olympiad, were successful by most of the standards
discussed by officials and the media. Los Angeles prospered
as much by what did not happen--terrorist attacks, traffic
jams, and smog sieges--as by what did take place--a well-
organized, profit-making sports festival with a record
number of spectators watching a record number of athletes
from a record number of countries.[1] At a time when many
observers viewed the Olympic movement as terminally ill,
the success at Los Angeles injected new vigor and spirit
into the Games. We will leave the post-1984 Olympic
prognosis for the final chapter. Now, though, let us
proceed to discuss the political anatomy of the Los Angeles
Games. We will be able to examine Olympic politics in

detail and in terms of a single Olympiad, neither of which was possible in the thematic and historical approach employed in Chapter Two's introduction to the politics of the Games. Our investigation will reveal that the Games of the XXIII Olympiad flourished both in spite of and because of surrounding political issues.

The success of the 1984 Games should not obscure the fact that the privilege of staging them was hardly a hot commodity. The IOC normally entertains lavish bids from several would-be host cities before bestowing on one of them the prize of putting on the Games. For 1984, though, the IOC received only one frugal offer to host the Olympics. The IOC first found itself in the unusual position of having to court other cities in search of more traditionally scaled bids, and then it discovered itself in the even more unusual position of not finding a properly extravagant suitor.

Consider the conditions of the Olympic movement and the state of Olympic hosts in 1977, the year the IOC received bids to stage the 1984 Games. Not only did the terrorist attack that killed 11 Israelis in the Munich Games tarnish the peaceful image West Germany worked so hard to present to a world that associated "Germany" with "Nazis," but the live global television coverage of the massacre graphically demonstrated that political statements made at this great political forum could now, through the miracle of modern technology, be instantly transmitted around the globe. In response, succeeding host cities would need to multiply the cost of security, in both manpower and dollars. Four years later, Montreal staged a Games devoid of terrorism but still full of politics, including the first large-scale Olympic boycott--30 African nations did not participate--and the nomenclatural rift between Canada and Taiwan that left athletes bearing the "Republic of China" name at home. Of greater concern to potential host cities were the costs of the 1976 Games--$1.5 billion in expenditures and a deficit surpassing $1 billion.[2] Eight years later, that deficit still exceeded $500 million.[3] Looking ahead from 1977, details about the 1980 Moscow Games were sketchy. Future Olympic hosts could be sure, though, that the prestige and propaganda value of the Games mattered far more to Soviet leaders than--and almost to the exclusion of--cost considerations. Moscow eventually carried Olympic extravagance to Olympian heights by spending an estimated $9 billion on its Games showcase.[4]

Cost control, then, was understandably paramount in the minds of the southern Californians working to return the Olympics to Los Angeles. An ongoing citizens' committee had labored toward this goal since 1939, seven years after the city hosted the Games of the X Olympiad. It was not until 1970, however, that the USOC picked Los Angeles as the official U.S. candidate to host the Games. The IOC received worldwide offers and, in 1970, selected Montreal as the 1976 host. In 1974, the IOC placed the 1980 Games in Moscow. It would receive bids for the 1984 Games through October 1977 and make its decision at its May 1978 meeting. But there was little to decide. The political and security problems--and the cost questions enveloping them--concerned Los Angeles but scared away other potential bidders. On October 31, 1977, IOC President Lord Killanin announced that Los Angeles was the only applicant for the 1984 Olympics.[5]

The key to Los Angeles's solution to the cost challenge was to turn the Games from a primarily civic enterprise into a largely private enterprise. Mayor Tom Bradley proposed a spartan Olympics, free from the extravagance that proliferated in previous Games. Bradley and his supporters were confident that fiscal prudence would allow the Olympics to be staged without a deficit. In any case, the city of Los Angeles would bear no financial liability for the Games. The organizing committee of the host city, generally associated with, if not an arm of, government, would have no such ties in Los Angeles. If Bradley and company were right about the profit-making potential of the Games, the private organizing committee would reap the benefits. If not, the committee would incur the losses. The city of Los Angeles would not.

The innovative Los Angeles concept was diametrically opposed to IOC philosophy. Previous Olympic hosts bore some responsibility for the continued lavishness of the Games, as cities and nations tried to outdo each other as well as present their political systems to the world in the most favorable light possible. Yet the IOC remained accountable for its share of what had become its luxurious athletic festival. IOC action has always been in the direction of "more"--more countries in the Olympic family, more sports on the agenda, more athletes participating in the Games, and more perks for IOC members. The prohibitive cost of integrating these expanded Olympic programs into an already expensive affair played a significant part in limiting bidders for the 1980 Games to Moscow and Los Angeles--each representing a superpower with extensive resources--and in the lack of competition for the 1984 award. The primary reason for the IOC's apparent ignorance of the difficulties in staging the Games is that it does not pay the bills. Rule 4 of the Olympic Charter requires that a host city assume financial liability for the Games.[6] The reconciliation of IOC attitudes, Los Angeles attitudes, and the Olympic Charter involved what the *Los Angeles Times* called "enough behind-the-scenes politicking to fill a couple of smoke-filled rooms."[7]

Stormy negotiations took place over the first several

months of 1978, with both Los Angeles and the IOC firm in their stands. When the city submitted its bid to the IOC, Bradley pledged to "conduct the Games in a spartan and businesslike manner" and to "avoid incurring the deficits which have plagued recent Olympic Games."[8] In January 1978, when the mayor presented a detailed Los Angeles proposal, he emphasized that it said "in clear language that if Los Angeles hosts the Games, we will control the costs."[9] The city was as serious about private funding as it was about its spartan concept; the Los Angeles bid had, in fact, been financed by the private Southern California Committee for the Olympic Games. Bradley needed to be firm if he wanted civic support. Several Los Angeles City Council members, skeptical of the promise of a deficit-free Olympics, persuaded the Council to place on the municipal ballot a measure forbidding any unreimbursed Games spending. Nor did critics fail to point out that voters in Denver rejected the 1976 Winter Games after the IOC had already awarded them to that city. For its part, the IOC showed no willingness to compromise. Killanin stated in March that, in whatever agreement was reached, Los Angeles would "assume complete financial responsibility."[10] After an April bargaining session between an IOC delegation led by Killanin and a Los Angeles group led by Bradley, the IOC's contract proposal still contained provisions leaving cost control with the IOC and fiscal liability with the city.[11]

No agreement had been reached by May, when the IOC was scheduled to choose a 1984 host city. The decision was both easy and hard, as Los Angeles was the only bidder but refused to agree to the terms of the Olympic Charter. The IOC voted to award the 1984 Games to Los Angeles on the condition that the city sign a contract on IOC terms. If no such agreement was approved by August 1, the IOC said it would revoke the award and accept new bids. This stand proved popular in the IOC, which wanted to publicly assert its sovereignty over the Games. Top members of the IOC knew privately, though, that its position was not practical. While negotiations between Olympic officials and Los Angeles stalled, the IOC had quietly searched for other bidders, but none could be found. Meanwhile, Bradley continued to insist that the city would not incur financial liability for the Games and thus could not agree to IOC terms that included acceptance of Rule 4. In addition, the mayor appointed a private, seven-member delegation to replace him in dealings with the IOC. This group would become the nucleus for the private Los Angeles Olympic Organizing Committee (LAOOC).

Bradley's committee did not capitulate on the mayor's primary concepts: a spartan, privately run Games involving no monetary risk on the city's part. New negotiations brought forth a plan that would become the foundation of the eventual agreement, calling for the private organizing

committee and the USOC to share financial responsibility
for the Games, thus absolving Los Angeles of any liability.
Holding steadfast to his rules, Killanin ignored the
private delegation and informed Bradley that the IOC
rejected the latest proposal because it did not conform to
Rule 4. The Los Angeles schemes all depended upon exemption
from that clause, but, after seven months of discussions,
Killanin and the IOC remained adamant about the city
agreeing to the IOC provisions of financial liability. On
July 18, a frustrated Bradley responded by recommending
that Los Angeles withdraw its bid to host the 1984 Games.

Bradley's action set in motion the final series of
events that brought the Olympics back to Los Angeles. The
mayor's call stunned the IOC. Killanin's group now faced
the dilemma of having nowhere to throw its party. In
addition, many cities interested in hosting the Games in
the future but wary of their costs were eager to see if the
Los Angeles idea would actually work. Sensing the IOC's
increasing isolation and lack of a viable alternative,
Killanin and the IOC resumed negotiations with Bradley's
private committee. Several weeks later, the IOC and Los
Angeles reached an agreement whose key conditions reflected
the mayor's original proposal and specifically exempted the
city from Rule 4. A private group would run the 1984 Games,
sharing financial liability with the USOC but not with Los
Angeles. On August 31, the executive board of the IOC
approved the contract, and the endorsement of the general
membership was announced on October 7. Five days later, the
Los Angeles City Council ratified the Olympic contract. The
IOC, USOC, and city officials signed the compacts on
October 20. As a final symbol of Los Angeles's victory,
city voters on November 7 passed the municipal charter
amendment prohibiting any unreimbursed Games outlays. The
taxpayers, like their mayor, wanted to stage the Games, but
not at civic expense; and the taxpayers, like their mayor,
got their wish.[12]

The magnitude of Los Angeles's triumph over the IOC
should not be underestimated. The IOC remains devoted to
ideals and especially to the idealism of its founder,
Coubertin, and presidents Brundage and Killanin have been
among the most faithful of the flock. Once the IOC
establishes rules, principles, or positions, it will not
budge from them until they become markedly divorced from
reality or unless it has no choice. For example, as noted
in Chapter Two, the IOC waited until 1968 to fully
recognize East Germany, bowing to political reality after
many world governments and sporting associations had long
since taken that step. In the Los Angeles case, the city
got the Games--essentially on its terms--only because the
IOC could not find a bidder that would accept its
conditions. Only when it became clear that the IOC would
either have to accept Los Angeles's way of staging the

Olympics or not have a 1984 Olympics at all did it select the former option. The latter choice, of course, would have been untenable for a body whose primary charge is to oversee and perpetuate the Olympic Games. Whatever the circumstances, Los Angeles achieved the rare distinction of forcing change upon a group not noted for welcoming it.

Beyond the politics of relations with the IOC, Los Angeles ventured onto oft-traveled political paths. To the LAOOC, the 1980 Moscow Games were the most recent and perhaps most thorough effort at using the Olympics as a world showcase for the political, economic, and social systems of the host country; the 1936 Berlin Games and 1964 Tokyo Games were but two of many similar endeavors. One might assume that having a private committee independent of government organize the Games would reduce the potential for such political manipulation, but the LAOOC operation ironically magnified that opportunity. "The L.A. Games," said Edwards, "are being widely hailed . . . as a showcase for illustrating the superiority of free enterprise as a strategy for Olympic and, by extension, national development."[13] Indeed, American ideology proclaims the virtues of capitalism, and U.S. foreign policy encourages other countries to adopt similar systems and strategies for economic growth. What better model could be found to demonstrate the worth of the American way than the Olympic Games? The success--or failure--of what was not unfairly called the "capitalist Olympics" would be seen by the entire world.[14]

The LAOOC was clearly aware of its heritage. The Los Angeles mission, as explained in an LAOOC handbook, was " . . . to operate an Olympic Games of the highest quality, and to realize a surplus of revenues over expenditures at the time of final accounting."[15] The second objective was no less important than the first, and LAOOC staff members were more aware of the latter goal in their day-to-day operations and planning, where cost factored heavily into every Olympic decision. One representative tale of the financial controls: negotiations between the Committee and Walt Disney Productions, the original producers of the multimillion-dollar opening ceremonies, broke down over the issue of who would pay for lunches for the thousands of participants involved.[16] Fiscal concern was foremost in the mind of the captain as well as his crew. LAOOC President Peter Ueberroth declared that his chief goal was to attain a surplus from the Olympics. "If I see it going the other way [toward a deficit]," stated Ueberroth, "I'll stop it. I won't be a part of it."[17] The LAOOC officially trumpeted its philosophy as "effective in pushing the Los Angeles Games toward a new standard of fiscal restraint, unheard of in prior Games."[18]

Such prudence was certainly unheard of in Moscow, where no expense was spared in staging the 1980 socialist showcase. One observer remarked that the Soviets appeared "genuinely peeved" that Ueberroth pointed out that Los Angeles would run its Games on a budget just 4 percent of Moscow's massive $9 billion outlay.[19] While government expenditures comprised almost all of Moscow's funding, Los Angeles banked on revenue from three primary sources: corporate sponsorship, broadcast rights fees, and ticket sales.[20] The organizers of the "capitalist Olympics" strongly emphasized the private financing of their Games at every opportunity for the benefit of the donors, still wary local taxpayers, and a world anxiously watching the Los Angeles experiment. The LAOOC's heralding of "the official opening of the quadrennial for the XXIII Olympiad" was highlighted by the announcement of the initial group of sponsors, "ushering in a new era of Olympic financing."[21]

The novelty of the private enterprise aspect of the 1984 Games was not lost on IOC President Juan Antonio Samaranch, who had replaced Killanin in 1980. "Los Angeles, in this case, represents the whole United States," said Samaranch, "and I think it will accept this challenge to organize the 1984 Games and to prove and to show what it is, what it represents, that is, the United States of America."[22] Although Samaranch is decidedly more realistic than his predecessors, Killanin and Brundage, this opinion is somewhat radical for the president of a still idealistic movement that believes its festival engenders global harmony. Samaranch seems to imply that a successful Los Angeles Games would prove the worth of the American system to a watching world. That kind of logic inspired Moscow's $9 billion spectacle. To be sure, many Los Angeles backers echoed Samaranch's sentiments, but such talk--even if it did acknowledge reality--was strange to hear from the mouth of an IOC president.

Nonetheless, the LAOOC took Samaranch's challenge to heart, and nowhere did Los Angeles "show what it represents" more than in the opening ceremonies. According to David Wolper, who replaced Disney as the producer of the ceremonies, a successful opening "sets the tone for the whole Olympic Games."[23] In planning "a show that would be majestic, inspirational, emotional--a 20-goose-bump experience,"[24] Wolper built on the excitement of such traditions as the march of the athletes and the lighting of the torch. Among the spectacular elements Wolper introduced were an awesome card stunt in which the flags of the world filled the mammoth Coliseum and an international television link that allowed people from Greece to France, from India to Italy, and from around the world to participate in a musical celebration of brotherhood.[25] The ceremony largely fulfilled its producer's plan to "uplift us, excite us, and get us ready for a joyous Olympic experience."[26]

Wolper's opening also got us ready for the flood of comparisons between the 1980 and 1984 Games. Because each

Olympics was staged by a superpower with a different
political system as well as a different method of
organizing and, in particular, financing the Games, such
comparisons were inevitable. But the Los Angeles ceremony
accelerated this trend and, in this respect, more than
realized Wolper's goal of establishing "the tone for the
whole Olympic Games." Ueberroth made an apt point in
elucidating ceremonial and societal contrasts between Los
Angeles and Moscow. "We don't have a society that allows us
to tell 30,000 people to practice for six months," noted
Ueberroth. "What we have to do is ask how many people want
to volunteer and then go to work for two or three weeks and
rehearse and put on a ceremonies."[27] The structure of the
opening reflected the United States; so, too, did the
content. "Past opening ceremonies," said Wolper, "have
traditionally celebrated what the host country gave to the
world in the way of culture, pageantry, and dance."[28] Since
U.S. music appeals to much of the world, a major segment of
the festivities featured a 3,000-performer musical history
of the United States, from George Gershwin to Duke
Ellington and from Irving Berlin to Michael Jackson.[29] "In
places," wrote Bill Shirley in the *Los Angeles Times*, "it
looked like an MGM or Warner Brothers musical."[30]

A brief history of the United States accompanied the
history of the country's music and evoked political
reaction. Trying to chronicle more than 200 years in about
an hour is a virtually impossible task, but Wolper's
attempt drew worldwide comment. Many of the reviews were
ideologically predictable--that is, Western nations liked
the ceremony, Eastern nations did not. Still, *Los Angeles
Times* writer Mike Littwin made a pithy observation: "The
show was vintage Hollywood, an old-fashioned, flag-waving
tribute to America as we want it to be."[31] Cuba's main
newspaper pointed out that Wolper's history ignored U.S.
mistreatment of blacks and native Americans.[32] And, asked
Michael Beglov of the Soviet news agency TASS, "What would
Americans have said had we opened the Moscow Games with a
celebration of the socialistic revolution?"[33]

Most viewers around the world--and many in the United
States--no doubt did not know or care about the details of
U.S. history. But more people--an estimated 2.5 billion--
would watch the opening ceremonies than any other televised
event ever held,[34] and the theme, not the specifics, of
what they saw prompted Jim Webster, an Australian
journalist and hence a relatively neutral observer, to make
one of many comparisons between Los Angeles and Moscow:

> The major difference that struck me between
> the two places was that here they used
> Americana, all painted and polished, to make
> the enormous impression they did. In Moscow,
> they used young people . . . to achieve their

> impressions. . . . It was neutral in its
> presentation. Not Soviet, but just young
> people who could have been from any
> background, any nation.[35]

In any event, Wolper achieved his ambition of setting "the
tone for the whole Olympic Games"--an American tone for a
Games run in distinctly American fashion and, on the field,
dominated by U.S. athletes.

An integral part of the opening ceremony was the
lighting of the Olympic flame. In 1936, the Berlin Games
organizers began the now traditional torch relay that
brings the flame from Olympia, Greece, the ancient home of
the Games, to the host city.[36] In its philosophy, the LAOOC
committed itself to use the Olympics to further the
development of youth in southern California and throughout
the United States, and the Los Angeles organizers saw the
torch relay as a vehicle for reaching that objective. The
LAOOC divided the route--a twisting 11-week journey across
the country--into segments called "Youth Legacy
Kilometers." For $3,000, one could buy the opportunity to
personally carry the Olympic torch for one kilometer or to
designate someone to do so. The millions of dollars raised
in the scheme would go not to the LAOOC but to
organizations like the Boys' Clubs of America, Girls' Clubs
of America, YMCA, and Special Olympics to expand athletic
programs for the youth of the United States.[37] The IOC,
although it had worried about possible
overcommercialization of the Olympics when it awarded them
to Los Angeles's private committee, did not consider the
Youth Legacy program overly commercial.[38]

The LAOOC was well under way with its sales when an
unlikely and virtually anonymous figure objected to the
Youth Legacy project. On January 30, 1984, the mayor of the
city of Olympia announced that he would bar the Olympic
flame from leaving his town if the torch relay was to
become a money-making event. "The Olympic flame is not a
dollar sign," declared Spyros Fotimos, "and we are
determined to prevent its overcommercialization."[39] The
LAOOC sent an emissary to Olympia to explain the torch
relay program, but Fotimos persisted in his protest. The
mayor garnered some support in Greece and forced the LAOOC,
Bradley, and even Samaranch into weeks of clarifications
and negotiations about the purpose and method of the fund
raising. Fotimos managed only to disrupt the planning of
the Greek start of the torch relay; the Youth Legacy
project and sales continued. With the IOC on Los Angeles's
side in the matter, it is difficult to envision any other
outcome.[40]

This episode merits mention here because it
demonstrates both the value and the relative ease of
Olympic political maneuvers. The Greeks who complained

about Games commercialism had only to look to their homeland for examples. The nation, for instance, sells Olympic commemorative coins, and Olympia itself has "shops that sell tacky Olympic souvenirs"[41] and the Olympic Flame Hotel.[42] Fotimos's motives also come into question, as the mayor's January 30 statement came more than six months after the LAOOC's initial announcement of its torch relay plans.[43] Apparently, no matter how faithful Fotimos seemed to be to his cause, his loyalty lay more with the Greek Communist Party than with the purity of the Olympic flame.

Fotimos, who moved to Olympia in 1982 in order to run for mayor, became the front man in a utilitarian and anti-American alliance between two leftist groups. When the Socialist Party came to power in 1981, it made three major promises: to pull Greece out of the North Atlantic Treaty Organization (NATO) and the European Economic Community (EEC), and to end the U.S. military presence in Greece. The Socialists, tempered by political reality, have not fulfilled any of those pledges; in fact, a 1983 agreement granted the United States a five-year extension on its military bases. The minority party Communists, unable to have any effect on NATO, the EEC, or the U.S. armed forces, focused a significant amount of protest on a domestic manifestation of the despised West: the Greek NOC. That body, generally regarded as conservative, has close ties with King Constantine, who was overthrown in a 1967 military coup. Constantine served on the IOC--which runs what was originally Greece's festival--from 1963 to 1974 and remains an honorary member today.[44] The Western orientation of the IOC, the rightist connections of the Greek NOC, and its perceived association with U.S. commercialism made the Greek body an "attractive target" for the Communists "seeking increased legitimacy."[45]

Meanwhile, the ruling Socialists seized the torch relay issue. After failing to implement their campaign vows, the Socialists joined the Communist crusade against the Greek NOC and the Los Angeles organizers to provide Greek citizens with a palpable sign of a publicly enduring anti-American attitude--a stance that helped propel the Socialists into office. Faced with the wrath of both the Socialists and Communists, the Greek NOC joined in the denunciation of the torch relay program rather than again draw political attention to itself. All of the Greek guns were thus fired at the LAOOC. If the target was the halt of the Youth Legacy project, then, as noted above, Fotimos and company failed. But neither the Communists nor the Socialists felt entirely frustrated. "The Communists achieved something by refusing to let the issue die," concluded David Lamb. "The government earned a bit of credibility with its radical critics."[46] The descendants of the original Olympians proved in 1984 that the torch could spark political as well as spiritual flames.

The political fire that had been lit by the Olympic flame had been extinguished, and the LAOOC organizers looked forward to May 8. On that day, the blazing torch would arrive in New York City, and the cross-country run to Los Angeles would begin. When May 8 arrived, thousands came out to greet the flame in New York. Cheers were mixed with tears as the grandchildren of two legendary U.S. Olympians, Jesse Owens and Jim Thorpe, carried the torch on the first segment of its journey. New York's enthusiastic reception for the Olympic flame--with the Games themselves still 11 weeks and 3,000 miles away--buoyed the spirits of the Los Angeles organizers. With its troubles with Fotimos over and the torch relay finally under way, the LAOOC looked forward to a brief bit of tranquillity before hitting the hectic home stretch of preparation.[47] Just two and a half hours later, that peace was shattered. In Moscow, the Soviet news agency TASS issued a statement that read in part: "The national Olympic committee of the USSR is compelled to declare that participation by Soviet sportsmen [in Los Angeles] is impossible."[48] The Olympic torch was on its way to Los Angeles; the Russians were not.

The Soviet boycott was the most visible of the numerous political maneuvers surrounding the 1984 Games and thus requires significant discussion here. As noted in Chapter Two, the Russians not only acknowledge but skillfully exploit the links between sport and politics. "The slogan 'sports have nothing to do with politics,' which is popular in the West, is not supported in the Soviet Union," reads a government pamphlet. "Sportsmen are ambassadors of peace. . . . We cannot take it seriously when somebody speaks of sport existing without any relation to politics."[49] The Russian viewpoint makes it virtually certain that the timing of the boycott announcement was precise, not coincidental. The popularity and accessibility of the Olympic stage allowed--indeed, inspired--the Soviets to snatch the lead role from the LAOOC on a day the Games would be in the global spotlight.

If the timing of the boycott statement was political, the statement itself was even more political. The single sentence above, part of a longer TASS press release, reveals much of Russia's strategy for attaining a positive reception for its announcement. The decision not to go to Los Angeles, TASS proclaimed and Soviet commentators repeated, was made by the Soviet NOC. If that committee was free from governmental influence, then the Russian implication that the Politburo had not made the decision might be credible. But, as Figure 1 showed, the state controls all aspects of Soviet sport.[50] The chairman of the Soviet NOC, Marat Gramov, previously served as the chief of the propaganda department of the Communist Party Central Committee.[51] The hand of the Soviet government was also apparent in the dismissal of Gramov's predecessor as NOC

head, Sergei Pavlov. If the Russian NOC did not have
political ties and its chairmanship was based primarily on
athletic experience, then Pavlov would have likely found
another sports job. Again, though, the state demonstrated
it had its NOC under its wing, as Pavlov found himself out
of the politically important Central Committee and into the
relatively insignificant position of ambassador to
Mongolia.[52]

Gramov's background would serve him well. The boycott
decision placed the Soviets in the lead role on the Olympic
stage, and they wanted good reviews from the world
audience. In trying to obtain those favorable reactions,
Gramov and the Russian propaganda machine emphasized two
themes in the TASS statement and subsequent campaign for
global support. First, as suggested in the above paragraph,
the Soviets attempted to define their action as a sporting
action and distinguish it from U.S.-USSR political
activity. This position was quite strange for Moscow to
adopt, given the Russian fondness for employing sport as a
tool of foreign policy. The Soviets, however, believed that
the world wanted to hear Moscow claim it would not mix
sport and politics. Second, the Soviets portrayed
themselves as victims, with U.S. politics forcing Russian
athletes to uphold Olympic ideals by staying home. Again,
Moscow made a pitch for world support.[53]

In trying to separate sport and politics, the TASS
statement went beyond asserting that the Soviet NOC, not
the Soviet government, was behind the boycott decision.
Exactly who would not attend the 1984 Games? TASS
explicitly said "Soviet *sportsmen*"[54] would not participate.
Later on May 8, a Russian official elaborated on his
country's attempt to separate sport and politics. Georgi
Arbatov, a member of the Central Committee and the director
of the United States and Canada Institute of the Soviet
Academy of Sciences, said the boycott "was not a sanction
for bad American foreign policy or the arms race that the
United States has imposed upon us. We consider it [the
Olympics] to be a sporting event."[55] Moscow also alleged
that the United States imposed the boycott on the Russians.
The TASS announcement did not say that the Soviet Union
chose to stay away from Los Angeles; instead, the Soviets
claimed they were "compelled to" do so. More important, the
Soviets did not use the word "boycott"; instead, they found
"participation" to be "impossible." This diction was
crucial in the Russian propaganda plan, where the United
States was continually attacked for violating Olympic
ideals. Gramov, the former propaganda chief, expounded on
this point three weeks before the boycott announcement.

> We will never boycott the Games. We support
> the rules and traditions of the Olympics.
> Such a word is not in our lexicon. In the

event that the Olympic Charter is fully observed, we will participate in the Games.[56]

The May 8 TASS statement provides a microcosm of the Soviet boycott plan and execution, but a more comprehensive analysis requires a more thorough investigation. The most prominent question to be answered is why Moscow spurned the 1984 Games. Unlike the situation in 1980, no single cause can be easily found for the Soviet action. The 1980 U.S. boycott decision was a reaction to the Russian invasion of Afghanistan. President Carter made that tie clear by asserting that, if Soviet troops made their way home, U.S. Olympians would make their way to Moscow.[57] In 1984, the Soviet Union wanted to stress its distancing of politics from sport as well as its championing of Olympic ideals. As opposed to Carter, then, the Soviet leadership could not present its boycott to the world as a foreign policy issue. "We could make it a sanction for [the U.S. invasion of] Grenada, let's say, or for . . . [the U.S.] mining of [the harbors of] Nicaragua," Arbatov told an American television audience. "But we don't have such a position."[58] As Gramov's comments indicated, the Russians felt the rationale for their decision needed to be closely related to the Olympic Charter.

Thus, the Soviet Union announced that worries about the security of its athletes would force them to stay home. Arbatov spoke of his nation's "concern for the safety and normal conditions for the athletes during this big event."[59] Before the boycott proclamation, Gramov said that "Soviet sportsmen must have normal conditions for participating in the Olympic Games."[60] Russian spokesmen assailed the LAOOC and the Reagan administration for "rude violations" of Olympic rules.[61] The theme of Moscow's explanations reflected a true party line; Arbatov used the phrase "normal conditions" seven times during his television appearance.[62] The Soviets were careful to emphasize that since the United States failed to satisfy reasonable safety concerns, Russia was compelled to defend peace and the Olympic Charter by not coming to Los Angeles. Further, the Soviets stressed that athletic performance, not international relations, was at the focus of their protest.

What, exactly, did the Soviet spokesmen mean by "normal conditions?" To interpret that phrase, of course, is to understand the rationale Moscow offered for its decision. "For a sportsman," said Arbatov, keeping the emphasis on athletic competition and trying to separate it from political rivalry, "it is important during such moments of strain to be in normal conditions, not harassed all the time by demonstrations, attempts to kidnap you or seduce you to leave your country, and all that sort of things."[63] The May 8 TASS release cited the existence of "extremist organizations and groupings of all sorts, openly aiming to create unbearable conditions for the . . . Soviet athletes."[64] After the boycott announcement, Gramov claimed that plans had been made to kidnap and drug Russian competitors.[65] In general, Moscow appeared to be worried about protestors disrupting the preparations and performances of its athletes and the possibility of defections for all the world to see.[66]

These charges of "anti-Soviet hysteria" were exactly what David Balsiger wanted to hear. Balsiger was the executive director of the Ban the Soviets Coalition, a group founded after a Russian missile downed a Korean Air Lines flight in September 1983, killing all 269 people aboard. The ultimate goal of Balsiger's organization was to fulfill its name and keep the Soviet team away from Los Angeles. To this end, the Coalition circulated petitions calling on the Reagan administration and the U.S. Congress to prohibit the Russians from entering the United States and the IOC to forbid them from participating in the Games.[67] If the coalition could not accomplish its primary objective, then it wanted to make life difficult for the Soviet athletes who did come to Los Angeles. The group sent many threatening letters to the Russian NOC, telling of plans for anti-Soviet propaganda to be spread by Coalition members on the LAOOC staff, for actively encouraging defections, and for establishing a network of sanctuaries to house any such defectors.[68] When Soviet spokesmen talked of extremism, of harassment, and of general "anti-Soviet hysteria," the Coalition was the primary target of Moscow's complaints. When the Russians revealed their boycott decision, Balsiger called May 8 "a great day for America," claiming that his group had "taken the greatest superpower in the world, in addition to the U.S., and a small coalition of citizens has stopped that country cold."[69]

Moscow alleged that the Reagan administration not only allowed but sponsored the Ban the Soviets Coalition and other anti-Soviet activities and demonstrations.[70] If the U.S. government indeed decided to ban the Soviets, the United States would violate the Olympic Charter by barring the representatives of an IOC-approved nation from entering the host country. Such a stance would substantiate a central part of Moscow's argument, the contention that the Soviets and not the Americans uphold Olympic ideals. Reagan, however, had guaranteed as early as 1981 that the United States would not prevent any Olympian from participation in Los Angeles, and the U.S. House of Representatives supported Reagan's declaration in a unanimous resolution in 1983.[71] In addition, the administration dissociated itself from the Coalition.[72] In its campaign, though, Russia implied that U.S. unwillingness to halt anti-Soviet activity inferred government collaboration with the Ban the Soviets Coalition and other groups with plans for political rallies.

The Ban the Soviets Coalition--and the Reagan administration's supposed approval of the organization-- received considerable exposure in the Soviet media. The group's statements and activities seemingly justified previous Russian criticism of the 1984 Games and provided a basis for future objections. "The Soviet media and Soviet Olympic officials have complained about the group," wrote journalist Maura Dolan, "and characterized its plans as examples of the kind of treatment the Soviets could expect in Los Angeles."[73] However, whatever propaganda value Moscow found in the Coalition, U.S. media and officials could not take seriously Soviet concerns about its schemes. The *Los Angeles Times*, for example, buried a story about the Coalition's plan to abet defections on page 34 of its news section.[74] Ueberroth viewed the organization as so inconsequential that "they could all get in a station wagon and drive south and it would be the end of it."[75] A U.S. State Department memorandum told the Soviets that "the publicity that the Soviet media has devoted to the Ban the Soviets Coalition has generated far more interest and U.S. press coverage of this insignificant group than it could have ever achieved on its own."[76]

It is true that U.S. officials would not forbid political demonstrations in Los Angeles. Such action would be indefensible under U.S. guarantees of freedom of speech and peaceful assembly. But the Soviets had little reason to feel threatened. Ueberroth noted that the Russians would not be the target of all the protestors. "They chant things against my mother outside," he said.[77] Whatever their content, rallies would not be allowed at the Olympic villages or venues.[78] After the unimpressed Soviets announced their boycott, Los Angeles Police Chief Daryl Gates gave his opinion of the Coalition and its possible impact on Games participants. "I respect that group's First Amendment right to do what they are doing," said Gates, "but I can tell you that the Russian athletes would never be aware of theirs or any other peaceful demonstrations."[79] Los Angeles organizers and U.S. officials were frustrated-- if not amused--at Moscow's stated rationale for the boycott. As Gates remarked, "I can't believe that the Russians would be intimidated by a tiny group like the Ban the Soviets Coalition."[80]

Gates was not alone in his disbelief. IOC President Samaranch discounted the Soviet allegations. The IOC, said Samaranch, was satisfied with the Los Angeles security plans.[81] Another Eastern nation, Romania, voiced its approval of the arrangements.[82] Even Cuba, which did join the boycott, anticipated no security problems at the Games.[83] The Russians seemingly had no solid ground on which to base a fear of defections. In fact, since the Soviets began Olympic competition in 1952, only one of

their athletes has defected, and he later returned
voluntarily.[84] Ueberroth wondered aloud why the Soviets did
not appear concerned about the welfare of the Russian
delegation of non-athletes--judges, NOC members,
journalists, and so forth--who would be coming to Los
Angeles.[85] Ueberroth did not accept Moscow's rationale at
face value, and he was correct. The foregoing discussion
elucidates the planning and implementation of Soviet
propaganda strategy for explaining the boycott to the
world. The roots of Moscow's decision, however, extend well
before the birth of the Ban the Soviets Coalition.

One of man's most basic motives lay behind the Soviet
boycott. That motive is revenge, and it was placed in the
collective Russian mind by the United States in 1980. As
pointed out in Chapter Two, Moscow viewed the 1980 Games as
a superb opportunity to showcase socialism to the world. By
awarding the Olympics to the Soviet Union, Russia told its
citizens and hoped to tell the world, the IOC and the
global community approved of socialism in general and of
Soviet foreign policy. But that message was never spread
internationally, because some 65 countries stayed away from
Moscow, most to protest Soviet action in Afghanistan. Not
only did the absence of so many national teams cause
Russian citizens to see beyond the party line on
Afghanistan and the Western boycott, much of the world
never witnessed the $9 billion Soviet spectacle.[86]

An embarrassed and angry Soviet Union then turned its
attention to the 1984 Games. By participating in them,
Russia would make the Los Angeles Olympics a probable
success. That outcome would enhance the global reputation
of the United States--the country most responsible for
damaging the glory of the 1980 Games. Even more disturbing
to the Soviets was the novel Los Angeles concept of staging
the Games; certainly, Moscow did not care to hear that the
private LAOOC would organize the 1984 Olympics for just 4
percent of the cost of the grand 1980 edition. Thus, the
Soviet Union's appearance in Los Angeles would help
demonstrate the virtues of free enterprise and help ensure
the success of the "capitalist Olympics" after the United
States had marred Russia's socialist showcase.

Despite numerous predictions between 1980 and 1984
that the Soviets would participate in the Los Angeles
Games, if only to defeat U.S. athletes on their home soil,
it is difficult in retrospect to see any compelling reason
why those forecasts were widely believed. Even before the
U.S. boycott plans were finalized, NBC sports chief Don
Ohlmeyer, who worked closely with Russian officials in
negotiating his network's arrangements for its planned
broadcast of the 1980 Games, warned that if the United
States pulled out of Moscow's Olympics, the Soviet Union
would do the same to Los Angeles.[87] In March 1980, Harry
Edwards spoke of the "virtual inevitability of a

retaliatory boycott."[88] After the hopes had been crushed and the Russian decision announced, U.S. officials acknowledged Jimmy Carter had much more impact on the Politburo than any Russian. "We are apparently paying the price for 1980," said Ueberroth.[89] One Soviet diplomat told the LAOOC president, "You sometimes call us the bear. . . . This time you can call us the elephant, because we don't forget."[90] Paul Conrad's *Los Angeles Times* cartoon (Figure 2) nicely summarized the Soviet boycott in Carter's eyeballs.

Revenge motivated the Soviets, then, as early as 1980. In their propaganda campaign of 1980, the Russians chastised the United States for leading a boycott, a weapon that Moscow insisted would never be employed by nations that upheld Olympic ideals.[91] The Soviets oiled their propaganda machine to try to deflect any cries of hypocrisy that might be directed at Moscow for staging a boycott of its own. As discussed earlier, Moscow wanted the world to regard a Soviet decision not to participate in the 1984 Games as a sporting, not a political, decision, taken reluctantly and only because the United States forced such action upon the Russians. Early development and consistent application of this propaganda framework made it possible for Arbatov to deny that the Soviet boycott was retaliatory in nature.[92] In fact, the establishment of a party line on the issue is evident in the striking comparison between Gramov's April 1984 comments[93] and the July 1980 remarks of Ignaty Novikov, who preceded both Gramov and Sergei Pavlov as NOC chairman. Just before the 1980 Games started, Novikov was asked if a Russian team would go to Los Angeles. "If we are invited, [and] if the United States does not violate IOC rules and regulations," replied Novikov, "we will accept with pleasure."[94] As a deputy premier, Novikov knew just how closely Moscow would scrutinize the behavior of the LAOOC and the U.S. government.

The IOC reacted to the possibility of a Soviet boycott in a surprisingly reasonable fashion. When Lord Killanin retired as IOC president in 1980, the body selected Juan Antonio Samaranch as its new leader. Samaranch had been as Spain's ambassador to the Soviet Union, and the IOC clearly hoped that his diplomatic rapport would help convince Moscow to send a team to Los Angeles.[95] While he opposed all boycotts--and indeed played a role in Spain's spurning the Western boycott in 1980--he acknowledged that "sport and politics did not live on separate planets."[96] Samaranch brought a refreshing dose of realism to a post and a body dominated by idealists and reactionaries. "It is very easy to say that politics and sports have nothing to do with each other," he observed. "But that's not true; the world is run by politicians."[97]

Despite his realistic nature, Samaranch would have no

FIGURE 2

AN EYE FOR AN EYE

impact on the Soviet politicians or on the plan they had devised. The Russian strategy was to periodically attack Los Angeles, being careful to point out potential hazards for Soviet athletes and possible breaches of the Olympic Charter. The Soviet newspaper *Izvestia*, for example, cited what it called a "confrontation between the interests of athletes and those of big business."[98] Other Russian grievances aired during 1981 and 1982 included Los Angeles smog, traffic, and crime problems that Moscow said would adversely affect its athletes, an alleged dearth of training facilities, excessive room and board charges, overcommercialization, and television control of event starting times.[99] In private meetings with Ueberroth, Soviet authorities maintained that the Russians would participate in the 1984 Games as long as the Olympic Charter was observed--the Soviet position all along.[100] In addition to laying the groundwork on which world sympathy might rest, Moscow had another reason for its maneuvering. By keeping attention focused on the supposed faults of the LAOOC and on the United States, Moscow would appear vindicated, not awkward, if a thaw in Soviet-American relations caused the Politburo to change its mind about attendance at Los Angeles. Russia could claim that it had brought the LAOOC and the United States into compliance with the Olympic Charter, proving the Soviet Union a far more worthy patron of the Olympic movement than the United States.

No such contingency came into play. The Soviets did keep the door of participation ajar by, among other actions, sending sports delegations to the United States, negotiating for Olympic television rights, and ordering tickets to the Los Angeles events. Yet the slander of the 1984 Games continued unabated in the Soviet press, and so did the deterioration of Soviet-American relations. The year 1983 brought the U.S. invasion of Grenada and the Russian attack on the Korean Air Lines plane, with each superpower condemning the action of the other. But the Soviets were primarily irked by the arrival and deployment of American Pershing 2 and cruise missiles in western Europe. Those occurrences prompted Russia's walking out of bilateral arms talks in Geneva and, for all of Moscow's propaganda about distinguishing sporting events from political issues, virtually ensured the Soviets would make good on their boycott threat.[101]

Many observers cited poor Soviet-American relations as a decisive reason why the Russians did not go to Los Angeles. Actually, the acrimonious atmosphere explained only why the Russians did not reverse their original stand on staying home in 1984. After the U.S. missiles arrived across the Atlantic Ocean, Soviet officials visited both their allies and western European nations, trying to discover which of the items on Moscow's long list of complaints about Los Angeles would be best received in Europe.[102] Those charges recurred in the Soviet press throughout late 1983 and early 1984, with Moscow eventually choosing to emphasize the security issue analyzed earlier in this chapter. Although the Russians mixed in hints that they would participate in the Games, and although several commentators speculated that the Soviet laments were meant primarily to gain concessions from the LAOOC and the U.S. government, Moscow's statements grew so vitriolic that journalist Robert Gillette was able to discern the Soviet strategy in November 1983. "As a contingency, Moscow appears to be laying the groundwork in its official press for later justifying a decision not to take part," wrote Gillette, who stopped just short of predicting a boycott. He also noted the Soviet attempt to avoid "the appearance of a political boycott," which would be hypocritical in light of Moscow's criticism of the West's action in 1980.[103]

The Soviet decision was virtually sealed in February 1984, when Konstantin Chernenko succeeded Yuri Andropov as premier of the Soviet Union. The accession of Chernenko effectively ended any thought of stopping the Soviet boycott plans and accompanying propaganda machine after four years. Chernenko was a top lieutenant of Leonid Brezhnev, the Russian leader most responsible for the socialist showcase in 1980 and thus most infuriated by the Western boycott. Ueberroth perceived that Chernenko, more than any other Soviet leader, was "the man who watched Brezhnev feel the pain of 1980."[104] Under the new premier, the Soviet boycott movement charged full speed ahead. Moscow accelerated the frequency and sharpened the tone of its criticisms of Los Angeles, and by April the U.S. State Department issued denials of Soviet charges on an almost daily basis.[105] On May 8, the Soviet Union finally made its well-planned and apparently well-timed announcement.

The Soviet propaganda machine then turned to the task of getting other countries to join the Russian boycott. Oft-appearing statements in the Soviet press attempted to justify both Moscow's decision and the stated reason for it. Moscow maintained its four-year-old positions of treating the boycott as a sporting, not a political, maneuver, and telling of the danger to Soviet athletes posed by LAOOC and U.S. violations of the Olympic Charter. The criticisms of the 1984 Games ranged from reasonable to incredible, with the latter adjective best describing two claims that Moscow hoped would help other nations see the hazards of Los Angeles. Gramov alleged that "methods have been devised for the abduction of Soviet people, for compelling them not to return to the motherland, for treating them with special drugs, including psychotropic preparations which destroy the nervous system."[106] In July, after a deranged James Huberty killed 21 people in a

McDonald's restaurant near San Diego, Moscow turned that tragic but isolated incident 130 miles from Los Angeles into an indictment of Olympic security and an ominous justification for the public rationale behind the boycott. "Gunfire is thundering on the eve of the Games," a TASS report read, "nightmarish testimony to the climate of violence reigning in the 'Olympic state.'"[107]

In trying to convince other nations to follow its lead, the Soviet Union employed other methods of propaganda besides plain rhetoric. The Russians covertly sent letters, purportedly from the Ku Klux Klan, to approximately 20 Asian and African countries planning to come to Los Angeles. The letters included such statements as "the Olympics--for whites only" and "We have forced the Soviets out of the Olympics. We shall not permit the apes to be present, either!" The notes were eventually exposed as KGB forgeries, and they were ineffective at that; none of the recipients decided to withdraw from the Games.[108] Eventually, 18 nations did not participate in the Los Angeles Games, with all but Iran, Albania, and Libya doing so in support of the Soviet boycott.[109] Moscow did not receive anywhere near the same level of backing that the United States did in 1980. Particularly notable was the presence of almost all black Africa at the Games, which we will soon discuss. The Russian strategy did not present the boycott as a response to a political event, as the United States did with Afghanistan, and so no sense of urgency prevailed among countries hearing the Soviet argument. Also, as pointed out earlier, many nations simply did not believe the Soviet charges about the dangers of Los Angeles. The Soviets actually did a reasonable job of implementing their boycott scheme. Moscow devised a decent plan to underscore the boycott that the Russians were determined to stage at any cost, and it is difficult to envision any other arguments the Soviet Union might have used in gaining greater global support.

The Russians' rhetoric about their respecting a distinction between sport and politics turned out to be particularly hollow. As we have seen, any boycott is a political act, and the Soviet one involved political revenge. Even more telling in exposing Moscow's flawed idealism was the status of most of the countries that supported the Soviet boycott. Overwhelmingly, those nations were Soviet allies, dependent on Moscow for economic and military assistance. Sport has a high priority with both the people and the governments in many of those countries, particularly East Germany, where every athletic triumph lends legitimacy to a state long denied recognition by the West. Olympic victory provides East Germany and other successful Eastern bloc states with a brief opportunity to escape from the Soviet shadow. Thus, most of the nations that supported Moscow did so reluctantly. The Soviet Union

does not treat dissenting allies pleasantly, and the
memories of the Russian invasions of Hungary in 1956 and
Czechoslovakia in 1968, as well as the threatened military
intervention in Poland in 1981, doubtless contributed to
eastern European decisions to endorse the Soviet boycott.
It is questionable whether Moscow would have employed
similar tactics to crush opposition to the boycott from a
key ally, but the Soviets could pull tightly on many
economic and military strings.

Romania did participate in the 1984 Games, and the
story behind that nation's appearance at Los Angeles gives
the biggest lie of all to the Soviets' propaganda about
their separating sport and politics. It was precisely
because of its political history that Romania, despite
being an eastern European and Warsaw Pact country, could
choose to snub the Soviet boycott. Romania's Olympic
conduct clearly reflected its foreign policy, which
Bucharest sets somewhat apart from Moscow. Bucharest
learned the lessons of Hungary, Czechoslovakia, and Poland
well, and internally Romania is a staunchly socialist
state, clamping down tightly on any domestic turmoil that
might cause Russia to use military force to keep Romania
within its grasp. Bucharest can thus feel secure in its
relatively independent foreign policy. Romania is the only
Warsaw Pact country that does not allow foreign troops on
its soil, Soviet or otherwise, and it is the only Warsaw
Pact nation that maintains diplomatic relations with
Israel. Romania also condemned Russia's invasions of
Czechoslovakia in 1968 and Afghanistan in 1979.[110] In each
of these instances, Bucharest knew how far it could stray
from the Soviet line without incurring the military wrath
of Moscow; sending a national team to Los Angeles was only
the latest in a series of such policy differences.[111]

The political value of having a Warsaw Pact nation in
Los Angeles, in the Games the Soviets wanted to see fail,
was not lost on Olympic officials. Despite public claims of
poverty throughout the pre-Games period, the LAOOC quietly
paid one-third of the cost of bringing the Romanian team to
Los Angeles. The IOC contributed another third.[112] In the
opening ceremony, only the home U.S. team got a louder
ovation than the Romanians, widely hailed by Americans for
defying the mighty Soviet Union.[113] During the Games, the
Romanians became a sentimental favorite among the
predominantly American spectators. By the end of the Games,
the Romanian team had collected 53 medals, the most ever
for the athletes of that country.[114] Those triumphs were
hailed in the Romanian press, surely contributing to
domestic tranquillity and allowing Bucharest further
expressions of its independent foreign stance.

The Soviet boycott was only one of three major reasons
why many observers predicted that African nations would
join the Eastern bloc in staying away from Los Angeles. A

change in the political strategy of those nations has occurred, and that shift will explain why black Africa participated in the 1984 Games despite quite reasonable expectations of an African boycott. Now, though, let us discuss what events seemed to dictate an African absence. Heading that list was the Soviet boycott. Moscow had been a staunch ally of black Africa's persistent efforts to keep South Africa out of the Olympic Games.[115] Some Olympic officials expected that loyalty would compel black Africa to support the Soviets in 1984.

Second, a South African national rugby team called the Springboks toured the United States in 1981. Although rugby is not an Olympic sport, matches between New Zealand and South Africa precipitated a 30-nation, predominantly black African boycott in 1976.[116] With that memory in mind, IOC, USOC, and LAOOC officials exhorted the U.S. government not to allow the Springboks into the country.[117] Those pleas were rejected, and the Reagan administration was charged with risking "the wrecking of an Olympics for the sake of three rugby matches."[118]

The third event that seemed to make black Africa's presence in Los Angeles a questionable proposition was the participation of Zola Budd. A 17-year-old South African girl, Budd ran a world record time in the 5,000 meters in January 1984. That mark went officially unrecognized, however, because the ruling body of track and field had banished South Africa in 1976.[119] None of its athletes can appear in the record books or compete in officially sanctioned meets, and the Olympics fall under that heading.[120] In order to compete against equally talented opponents and take part in the Olympics, Budd applied for British citizenship. Since her father and grandfather were British subjects, Budd's request was approved.[121] Many incensed black African nations did not see Budd as an English woman but as a South African wearing the Union Jack for show, and LAOOC General Manager Harry Usher surmised that a boycott of approximately 20 countries might result.[122]

Since the last two episodes particularly seemed to undermine the goal of isolating South Africa in international sport, the anticipation of a 1984 black African boycott was warranted. Why did black Africa change its approach from 1976? Those nations, comprising much of the Third World, try to maintain nonaligned status, not pledging unconditional loyalty to either the United States and the Western alliance or to the Soviet Union and the Eastern bloc. Hence, black Africa would not blindly follow Moscow's lead in boycotting the 1984 Games. Given that most of these countries have been relatively recently liberated from their colonial past, their paramount interest in independence is understandable. The primary factor in Third World policy making is self-interest.

It is black Africa's perception of its self-interest, then, that has changed since 1976. Those nations have come to understand that while an Olympic boycott remains a meaningful political statement, participation in the Games offers countries access to a global political forum almost unparalleled in its reach. In addition, athletic triumphs provide black African nations, many of which are small and young, with instant worldwide attention otherwise hard to obtain.[123] "Sporting achievements," says Nigerian Minister of Sport Sylvanus Williams, "today are used as a measure of our country's greatness."[124] Having largely succeeded in isolating South Africa in international sport, the black African nations threatened to isolate themselves through their Olympic boycott strategy.[125]

The unwillingness to stay away from Los Angeles over the Springbok and Zola Budd issues does not mean that black Africa has eased its campaign to quarantine South Africa in international sport in hopes of ending racial segregation and discrimination in that country. The goal stays the same; the tactics have changed. Black Africa has won numerous battles in international sports federations, many of which have, like the IOC, suspended or banned South Africa.[126] That country has been left with markedly decreasing opportunities for international athletic competition, and black Africa has responded by targeting countries that maintain sporting links with South Africa.

Thus, in the wake of a 1979 rugby exchange between Britain and South Africa, the Supreme Council for Sport in Africa (SCSA), the body that called the 1976 black African boycott, did not consider the Olympics in devising a response. Instead of calling on the IOC to suspend England or on the black African countries to boycott the 1980 Games, the SCSA voted to "ban all bilateral sporting links with Britain [and] not to support British members in international organizations."[127] Similarly, the 1984 Games were not threatened by the Springbok tour or Zola Budd. The SCSA protested to the United States in the former case and Britain in the latter, encouraging other countries to follow suit. Black Africa's fight to force change in South Africa's racial policies continues, and, despite the modified Olympic strategy, sport remains a valuable weapon in that battle.

The Soviet boycott, while providing a measure of revenge for 1980, did not ruin the Los Angeles Games. Politically, the boycott ignited what was already a fire of U.S. nationalism into an inferno. Even before the Soviet announcement, advertisements appearing with regularity and with urgency in national publications exhorted Americans to contribute money toward the success of the U.S. team in Los Angeles. Repeatedly, though, these appeals ignored any Olympic spirit of sportsmanship, because the concept of success pitched to U.S. citizens could be achieved only through the concomitant failure of the athletes of other nations.[128] The USOC approved a Miller Beer fund-raising campaign that had as its slogan, "Let's Win the Games Again."[129] A bank advertisement urged readers to contribute money to the U.S. Olympic team, thus "helping America win the 1984 Olympics." In return for their donation, contributors received a record album entitled *Great Songs of America for the U.S. Olympic Team.* The songs were American, the athletes were American, and the spokesman-- Bob Hope, who entertained U.S. troops overseas in several wars--was quintessentially American. Even the Olympic flame, appearing on the red, white, and blue album cover, was subsumed into Americana.[130]

The nationalism grew significantly with the Soviet boycott. Moscow may have prided itself on upstaging the start of the cross-country torch relay with the boycott announcement, but the timing that seemed brilliant to the Politburo backfired as the Olympic flame moved west. The torch became transformed from an Olympic symbol to an American symbol, and the throngs who came out throughout the United States to view the flame turned its passing into spontaneous demonstrations of pro-U.S., anti-Soviet statement. Richard Sargent, an LAOOC aide who accompanied the relay, recalled that "we'd see signs [held up in the crowds] . . . 'To hell with the Russians' and 'Go America' and that kind of stuff."[131] As the large gatherings across the United States continually expressed such nationalistic feelings, 1972 Olympian Jon Andersen was compelled to ask, "Do we need to be reminded that the torch doesn't represent the United States, that it's a symbol for *all* nations and people in the world?"[132] The answer was yes, but reaction to the Soviet boycott drowned out Anderson's message.

As the start of the Games and the arrival of the torch edged closer, the excitement and nationalism in Los Angeles reached a fever pitch. The prevailing U.S. attitude seemed to be "We'll show them," demonstrating to the Soviets not only how to run an Olympics but also how to do well in them. "Let the Russians Play With Themselves," read a popular button.[133] These sentiments were not confined to the popular masses of the United States. Witness this excerpt from an Olympic preview, written by a director of the USOC in an official USOC publication:

> The question of whether the Soviet Union is amateur or not should now be settled once and for all as their athletes sit and watch the rest of the world go by in Los Angeles. The Russians are very definitely amateurs at staging a boycott of the Olympic Games.
> Wrapping a blatant political and revenge-motivated decision in the Olympic banner, the Soviets have decided to pass on

this Olympic Games, carping about security,
"safety" of athletes and officials, smog,
food, housing, anti-Soviet groups, and the
whole menu of garbage that they expect the
world to buy.[134]

Anti-Soviet propaganda combined with pro-American
passion. Spectators found an official "Olympic Cheering
Card" inside their program. The letters "USA" appeared on
the placard in red, white, and blue, and fans were
instructed to "show your colors with pride" by waving the
card "proudly for all the world to see." It was of little
concern to Olympic sponsors if some spectators did not
happen to be Americans or did not plan to root incessantly
for the home team.[135] Those fans who did pull for U.S.
athletes were seldom disappointed. U.S. competitors
captured 174 medals, three times the number of the next
most successful team, and won an Olympic record 83 gold
medals.[136] The victory orgy on the field and in the
American media prompted Howard Rosenberg to ask, "What has
happened to all those lovely words about the act of
participation being more important than medals? Why must
the gold medal count be the lead story on so many
newscasts? Why is it imperative that we must always
win?"[137] American culture, with its emphasis on winning,
encouraged such an approach, and the Soviet boycott
intensified the U.S. desire to show the Russians just how
much fun the Olympics could be, and how nicely they could
be run, without the Soviets. Even the *Los Angeles Times*,
which included in its Olympic coverage a forum of praise
and criticism from around the world, succumbed to the
nationalistic spirit by running a chart celebrating U.S.
domination by comparing the number of gold medals the
United States could have won in each sport with the number
that it did.[138]

Both Ueberroth and Usher admitted that the Soviet
boycott was a significant catalyst in the successful
operation of the 1984 Games.[139] The "We'll show them"
attitude infected Olympic staff as well as the American
public, although LAOOC personnel displayed their feelings
in a more diplomatic manner. But, if the Soviet boycott did
not wreck the Los Angeles Games, it did provide fuel for
the Russian propaganda campaign that persisted throughout
the Games. Among the most common complaints about Los
Angeles in the Soviet press were the excessive displays of
U.S. nationalism and the allegedly meaningless domination
of U.S. athletes. The Soviets inspired both criticisms
themselves. The boycott announcement could not have been
any better timed for the purpose of promoting U.S.
nationalism, and the Eastern bloc withdrawal pulled two of
the world's three major sports powers--the Soviet Union and
East Germany--out of the 1984 Games. U.S. athletes could

not help but reap the resulting harvest of medals. Hence, although the Los Angeles Games were globally perceived as successful, the Soviet boycott did have an effect in Russia. The boycott fulfilled Moscow's desire for revenge, and its aftermath allowed--indeed, caused--the Soviets to further disparage the 1984 Olympics.

Amid all the talk of nations that did not show up in Los Angeles, one very important nation did--the People's Republic of China. The participation of the PRC athletes-- and Taiwanese athletes--in 1984 culminated an Olympic struggle over political legitimacy as old as the PRC itself. After the Long March and 1949 establishment of the People's Republic, the Nationalist Chinese fled to Taiwan, from where they insisted that they still ruled the Republic of China. Avery Brundage saw China, like Germany, as one nation and wanted a joint Chinese team to compete in the Games.[140] Unlike the German situation, though, neither the PRC nor the ROC would discuss a unified squad. Each regarded itself the sole legitimate government of China, and a combined team would do nothing for either regime's claim of national jurisdiction.[141]

Unable to achieve joint PRC-NOC participation, the IOC in 1954 decided that two Chinas existed by recognizing the NOC of each. This judgment did not please either side, particularly the PRC, which would not stay in the Olympic family as long as it recognized the ROC. Brundage, who attained the IOC presidency in 1952, did not enjoy cordial relations with the representatives of mainland China, one of whom called him "a faithful menial of U.S. imperialists."[142] This persistently hostile atmosphere and the IOC's two-China policy prompted the PRC to withdraw from the Olympic family--and from many international sport federations--in 1959.[143] Twenty-five years later, an official publication by the NOC of the PRC bears witness to the relationship between sport and politics and the stand that the PRC has consistently taken since 1959. According to that NOC, "to safeguard China's state sovereignty and uphold the Olympic Charter, the COC had no alternative but . . . to suspend its relations with the IOC."[144] The IOC also decided that Taiwanese athletes could no longer bear the name of the "Republic of China," since the Nationalist government did not control mainland China.[145] Although Taiwan did compete as "Formosa" in the 1960 Rome Games, the nomenclature issue subsequently subsided with the PRC out of the Olympics entirely.[146]

Several significant factors combined over the following two decades to return the PRC to the Olympic movement. A distinctly political thread ran through most of these factors. First, the world consensus regarding Chinese legitimacy had shifted. It was the PRC, not the Nationalists on Taiwan, that most countries and the United Nations now viewed as the true government of China. Second, the death of Mao Zedong ushered in a fresh and somewhat less rigid leadership in the PRC. Third, and most important, the United States acknowledged political reality in 1979 by conferring diplomatic recognition upon the PRC and simultaneously withdrawing it from Taiwan. The U.S. decision removed the last pin holding in place any measure of international agreement with Taiwan's claim to be the legitimate Chinese government.[147]

Canada's refusal to let Taiwanese athletes into the country to compete in the 1976 Montreal Games under the ROC name, although embarrassing to the IOC, foretold the eventual resolution of the China issue.[148] Lord Killanin, who replaced Brundage in 1972, was committed to including the PRC in the Olympics. Killanin had worked in mainland China, and in any case he could not fail to have a warmer relationship with the country and its leaders than Brundage did.[149] Besides, pointed out the PRC and its allies, a truly global event could not continue to leave out almost one-fourth of the world's population.[150] Amazingly, the IOC in 1979 offered to sponsor discussions regarding a joint Chinese team, an option rejected in 1954 and, not surprisingly, spurned again 25 years later.[151] Other efforts at a negotiated agreement also failed.

The PRC, though, had subtly changed its position. Beijing's new leaders no longer insisted that Taiwan be expelled from the Olympic movement in order for the PRC to rejoin. Instead, Beijing demanded that Taiwan drop the name "Republic of China" and all references to its being the sole legitimate Chinese government. This concession was enough to satisfy an IOC already receptive to PRC membership. In November 1979, the IOC voted overwhelmingly to admit the PRC as the Chinese Olympic representative. If Taiwan did not change name, flag, and anthem--all of which conveyed the impression of Taiwanese control over all of China--for Olympic purposes, then the IOC would suspend the country effective January 1, 1980.[152] Changing global political reality and limited PRC flexibility had given Beijing what it wanted.

An angry Taiwan vowed to fight the edict. It filed lawsuits against the IOC in Switzerland, the home of the IOC, and the United States, which was hosting the 1980 Winter Games at Lake Placid. Initially, the Swiss courts rejected Taiwan's claim that the IOC did not have the power to make its judgment. In the United States, Taiwan's somewhat more sound contention that its constitutional rights were being violated resulted in sympathy but not victory.[153] Forced out of the Winter Games, Taiwan's pride in its claim of legitimacy, now denied by the rest of the world, compelled a boycott of the Moscow Summer Games as a self-respecting but meek protest. Despite public pronouncements, of course, the suspension imposed on Taiwan meant that it could not have participated in the Summer

Games even if it had so desired. Meanwhile, despite the anticipation of its first Olympic participation in more than three decades, the PRC joined the 1980 U.S. boycott. "After fighting for years to get both Chinas into the Olympics," wrote journalist Bill Shirley," the IOC ended up with neither."[154]

The 1984 Games would mark the conclusion of the China chapter in IOC affairs. Having finally devised a solution by which both the PRC and Taiwan would participate in the Games, the IOC was understandably eager to implement its plan. The PRC would pose no problem; the newly established diplomatic relations between the United States and the PRC assured its presence in Los Angeles. Taiwan, however, still bristled at the conditions the IOC had imposed in its 1979 decision. But this discontent gradually took second place behind *realpolitik* in Taiwan's evaluation of the situation. Taiwan came to realize that Olympic participation, under whatever name, conferred a sense of legitimacy that was increasingly eroding in other world forums. In addition, Taiwan acknowledged what black Africa already understood: the Olympic stage could be used most effectively by those countries taking part in the Games. In 1981, Taiwan agreed to the IOC's conditions for reinstatement. In Olympic matters, the Republic of China thus became Chinese Taipei, with a new flag and anthem. Taiwan also dropped its still pending legal action against the IOC in Swiss courts.[155] The agreement did nothing to alter the PRC's contention that it ruled all of China, and Chinese Olympic guides pointedly referred to Taiwan's NOC as "an Olympic committee for China's Taiwan region."[156] Both PRC and Taiwanese athletes competed in Los Angeles.

So did the athletes of 140 other nations. From the U.S. contingent of 597 participants to the Bangladesh delegation of one, the Games of the XXIII Olympiad became a party as well as a sports festival. Although two of the three world's major athletic powers stayed home, once the Games finally got under way, complaints from those who were not there became lost in compliments from those who were. The 1984 Olympics were not perfect, but--as black Africa and Taiwan realized--capturing world attention during the Games requires attending them. An Austrian newspaper concluded:

> The Soviet boycott appeared to degrade the Games even more than the non-participation of the West at Moscow in 1980. But those who aren't there can't win, and nobody misses them either. The Americans made the best of the competition and Olympia won once again.[157]

Yet, for all the politics that both contributed to and

detracted from Los Angeles's success, another issue reared
its head after the conclusion of the Games, a topic
involving global politics and internal LAOOC politics.

When Los Angeles signed its contract with the IOC in
1978, the agreement was based on the assumption that the
1984 Games could be staged without incurring a deficit. Los
Angeles taxpayers had made it clear that they would welcome
the Games with open arms but not open wallets.[158]
Accordingly, no matter what else might happen in sports or
political arenas, the 1984 Olympics would be perceived as a
failure if the objective of a deficit-free Games was not
achieved.[159] Ueberroth and the LAOOC responded to that
challenge by turning it from a goal into a mission, with
all of the zeal that the word implies.

The primary goal of the 1984 Games was to avoid losing
money, more so than to make money. Ueberroth did an
admirable job of keeping the LAOOC attuned to the challenge
of putting on a deficit-free Olympics. He and LAOOC
spokesmen continually presented projections of a $15
million surplus from $513 million in revenues. With this
apparent 3.5 percent margin, all that stood between fiscal
solvency and the dreaded deficit, the bottom line took top
priority and loomed over negotiations with state and local
governments, suppliers, and contractors as well as over the
work of the LAOOC staff. Ueberroth and company continually
pleaded poverty in haggling with municipalities over
reimbursements for security expenses, with trade unions
over construction costs, and with LAOOC staffers over
virtually any outlay. The LAOOC told the Southern
California Rapid Transit District (RTD) that no money could
be provided to subsidize Olympic bus service. Ueberroth and
LAOOC management constantly reminded workers that even
seemingly small expenses could spiral. Supplying lunches to
volunteers, Ueberroth was fond of saying, would eat up half
of the projected surplus.[160]

As the Olympics grew nearer, murmurs that the LAOOC
would make far more than $15 million became loud rumors.
Ueberroth publicly called such speculation "absolutely
inaccurate,"[161] and the LAOOC staff and board of directors
heard the same message. Only three men at the LAOOC--
Ueberroth, General Manager Harry Usher, and James Mitchell,
the finance chief--knew the complete fiscal picture, and it
became clear to them that the image grew rosier as the
Games approached. The $15 million estimate greatly
underestimated revenues, particularly from ticket sales,
and included unpublicized contingency money for a series of
calamities. This unlikely sequence of adversity never
occurred, and neither did any of its components. Early in
1984, Ueberroth and Usher knew the surplus would be many
times larger than $15 million but kept up the hard
financial line to the public, the IOC, and their own
staff.[162] On September 11, one month after the Games ended,

Ueberroth told a startled world that the LAOOC now projected a $150 million surplus.[163] In the end, the 1984 Olympics turned a profit of $222 million on revenues of $718 million.[164]

Los Angeles organizers had promised free enterprise, and it worked--perhaps too well. The windfall upset those who dealt with a chronically frugal LAOOC and those who did not wish to see the Games as a profit-making venture. Many LAOOC staff members, although satisfied at achieving the goal of a deficit-free Olympics, generally did not see a valid reason for misleading the staff about the financial situation or for scrutinizing expenditures so tightly. The 50,000 LAOOC volunteers certainly must have wondered why they could not receive a stipend, let alone a salary. A liaison between one of the venues and the LAOOC termed the surplus "obscene."[165] An official of the city of Los Angeles called the profit "a shrine Peter Ueberroth built to himself."[166] The IOC was reported to be "shocked."[167]

Despite the fact that a private committee ran the 1984 Games, the disposition of the surplus would reflect on the United States. The first use of Olympic profit truly reflected corporate America. The LAOOC board of directors awarded bonuses to 6,500 employees--less than 10 percent of the Games work force--ranging from $500 to $350,000 for Usher and $475,000 for Ueberroth.[168] Meanwhile, the LAOOC denied the RTD's request to help retire its $5 million deficit for Olympic bus service.[169] Paul Conrad's cartoon (Figure 3) depicted winners and losers in post-Olympics financial awards. As the LAOOC continued to turn down requests for money, the world watched in amazement as the surplus expanded even after the Games ended. Interest payments alone added $2 million per month to the profits.[170]

Officially, Samaranch was "surprised" at the large surplus.[171] He and Ueberroth presented the LAOOC with a proposal to allot a modest $7 million of the profit to reimburse NOCs for housing expenses, with each NOC's share of the money proportional to the size of its national team.[172] Ueberroth noted that one reason for the Games' success was that many countries increased the size of their delegations at the LAOOC's request, and at considerable cost, to make up for the absence of Eastern bloc athletes.[173] He called the $7 million a "legacy",[174] and Samaranch termed it a "gesture."[175] Since the 1978 contract made the LAOOC and USOC financial partners in staging the Olympics, both groups had to agree on any initial disbursement of the profit. The LAOOC approved the reimbursement scheme, but the USOC did not. The USOC contended that since foreign governments control many NOCs, athletes would not be likely to benefit from the funds.[176] Whatever the validity of that logic might be, the USOC vote did not leave U.S. friends or foes with a positive

FIGURE 3

connotation of the moniker "capitalist Olympics."[177]

Nobody wanted to stage the 1984 Games, but many wanted to criticize or disrupt them. To some extent, as documented in this chapter, they succeeded. Much more impressive is the fact that Los Angeles succeeded as well. The LAOOC overcame many obstacles--some of which are noted in the observation that opens this chapter--and we will turn our attention to the significance of that victory in Chapter Four. For the moment, though, let us remember the 1984 Games as most people will--in economic terms. Perhaps above all, the words "deficit" and "surplus" were associated with these Games. The final comment in this chapter will rest with a journalist who covered the Los Angeles Games from the 1977 bid through the disposition of the surplus. IOC rules require the Olympic organizers to publish a final report, and the LAOOC announced in December 1984 that the public was welcome to buy a copy--at $550 each. "To the end," wrote Kenneth Reich, "the Los Angeles Games represent both the bright and the dark sides of [the] free enterprise system."[178]

NOTES

Epigram 1: Harry Edwards (1984), p. 46.

Epigram 2: Quoted in *Sports Illustrated*, August 27, 1984. The speaker is unnamed.

1. Surprising as it may seem, these numbers are in dispute. The sources used here are as follows: spectators--LAOOC (1984e); athletes--LAOOC (1984c), p. 4; nations--*Los Angeles Times*, August 2, 1985.

2. Edwards (1984), p. 46.

3. *Los Angeles Times*, July 23, 1984.

4. *Sports Illustrated*, March 5, 1984.

5. LAOOC (1984a), p. 108, and *Los Angeles Times*, July 30, 1984.

6. LAOOC (1984a), p. 28.

7. *Los Angeles Times*, July 30, 1984.

8. Quoted in *Los Angeles Times*, February 22, 1981.

9. Quoted in *Los Angeles Times*, July 30, 1984.

10. Ibid.

11. LAOOC (1984a), pp. 27-28, and *Los Angeles Times*, July 30, 1984.

12. LAOOC (1984a), pp. 27-29, 108, and *Los Angeles Times*, July 30, 1984.

13. Edwards (1984), p. 44.

14. Ibid.

15. LAOOC (1984a), p. 50.

16. *Los Angeles Times*, July 31, 1985.

17. Quoted in *Sports Illustrated*, March 5, 1984.

18. LAOOC (1984a), p. 31.

19. *Los Angeles Times*, November 14, 1982. The observer

is veteran Olympic reporter Kenneth Reich.
20. LAOOC (1984a), p. 50.
21. LAOOC (1984a), p. 109.
22. Quoted in *Los Angeles Times*, August 3, 1980.
23. Quoted in *Los Angeles Times*, July 26, 1984.
24. Quoted in LAOOC (1984c), p. 14.
25. LAOOC (1984c), p. 27.
26. Quoted in LAOOC (1984c), p. 14.
27. Quoted on "Olympic Report," KALX, July 27, 1984.
28. Quoted in LAOOC (1984c), p. 14.
29. LAOOC (1984c), pp. 14-24.
30. *Los Angeles Times*, July 29, 1984.
31. Ibid.
32. *Los Angeles Times*, July 30, 1984. Many history textbooks in the United States also gloss over these areas.
33. Quoted in *Los Angeles Times*, August 9, 1984.
34. LAOOC (1984c), p. 13.
35. Quoted in *Los Angeles Times*, July 31, 1984.
36. LAOOC (1984a), p. 92.
37. LAOOC (1984a), pp. 90-91. Also see pp. 96-103 regarding the LAOOC's youth philosophy and programs.
38. *Sports Illustrated*, February 27, 1984.
39. Quoted in *Los Angeles Times*, January 31, 1984.
40. See, for instance, *Sports Illustrated*, February 27, 1984; and *Los Angeles Times*, February 17, 1984; February 22, 1984; March 21, 1984; April 27, 1984; April 29, 1984.
41. *Los Angeles Times*, May 7, 1984.
42. *Los Angeles Times*, February 17, 1984.
43. An LAOOC press conference explained the torch relay program on July 28, 1983. (LAOOC [1984a], p. 91)
44. Guttmann, p. 270, and *Los Angeles Times*, May 7, 1984.
45. *Los Angeles Times*, May 7, 1984. Leftist extremists are suspected of assassinating Greek NOC President Georges Athanassiadis in 1983. No one has been convicted of the murder.
46. *Los Angeles Times*, May 7, 1984. Much of this discussion is adapted from David Lamb's cogent analysis in that issue.
47. *Los Angeles Times*, May 9, 1984.
48. Quoted in *Los Angeles Times*, May 9, 1984.
49. Quoted in Hazan, p. 205.
50. It is helpful to recall here that an NOC need not be part of the government machinery for a country to boycott an Olympics. The Carter administration, not the USOC, was behind the U.S. decision to stay away from the 1980 Games.
51. *Los Angeles Times*, February 8, 1984.
52. *Los Angeles Times*, January 15, 1983.
53. Hazan notes that the Soviets are as relativistic as any other nation with regard to sport and politics. In

Chapter One, we saw the pronounced links between those two spheres in Soviet society, and Chapter Two showed that the Russians have been as active in Olympic politics as any other country. In 1980, though, "the Soviet propaganda apparatus" tried to counter the Western boycott by stressing "two main motifs: (1) sport and politics are separate and should not be mixed; and (2) the United States invented the sports boycott as a political instrument." The discussion in Chapter Two makes clear that the Soviet propaganda continually distorts reality. The Soviets, however, must have found some sympathy for their rhetoric; as the text demonstrates, they used similar themes in their 1984 propaganda. (Hazan, pp. 204-205)

54. Emphasis added.
55. Quoted on *Nightline*, May 8, 1984.
56. Quoted in *Los Angeles Times*, April 17, 1984.
57. Kanin, pp. 119-121.
58. Quoted on *Nightline*, May 8, 1984.
59. Ibid.
60. Quoted in *Los Angeles Times*, April 17, 1984.
61. Quoted in *Los Angeles Times*, May 9, 1984. The speakers are unnamed.
62. Quoted on *Nightline*, May 8, 1984.
63. Ibid.
64. Quoted in *Los Angeles Times*, May 9, 1984.
65. *Los Angeles Times*, May 15, 1984.
66. *Los Angeles Times*, November 3, 1983.
67. *Los Angeles Times*, September 27, 1983.
68. *Los Angeles Times*, November 2, 1983; March 18, 1984; April 25, 1984.
69. Quoted in *Los Angeles Times*, May 9, 1984.
70. See, for example, *Los Angeles Times*, November 3, 1983; April 17, 1984.
71. LAOOC (1984a), pp. 32-33, 122. In the wake of the Korean Air Lines incident, the California state legislature voted to ask Reagan to ban Soviet athletes from entering the United States. The resolution was later rescinded and replaced by a declaration calling on Reagan, Congress, and all Californians to welcome Olympians from all countries. (*Los Angeles Times*, September 25, 1983; March 1, 1984; March 16, 1984)
72. *Nightline*, May 8, 1984.
73. *Los Angeles Times*, May 9, 1984.
74. *Los Angeles Times*, March 18, 1984.
75. *Los Angeles Times*, May 21, 1984.
76. Ibid. The memorandum was sent before the boycott was announced.
77. Quoted on *Nightline*, May 8, 1984.
78. *Nightline*, May 8, 1984.
79. Quoted in *Los Angeles Times*, May 9, 1984.
80. Ibid.
81. *Los Angeles Times*, May 19, 1984.

82. *Sports Illustrated*, July 2, 1984.
83. *Los Angeles Times*, June 8, 1984.
84. *Los Angeles Times*, April 19, 1984.
85. *Los Angeles Times*, May 19, 1984.
86. Kanin, p. 145.
87. *Los Angeles Times*, January 9, 1984.
88. Quoted in *Los Angeles Times*, March 9, 1980.
89. Quoted in *Los Angeles Times*, May 9, 1984.
90. Quoted in *Sports Illustrated*, May 21, 1984.
91. Another example of relativism in Olympic politics: an official Soviet history of the Olympics applauded those who boycotted the 1936 Berlin Games to protest the Nazi regime. Fascism, of course, is even more antithetical to socialism than is Western democracy. (*Los Angeles Times*, May 4, 1980)
92. *Nightline*, May 8, 1984.
93. See page 48.
94. Quoted in *Los Angeles Times*, July 16, 1980.
95. *Los Angeles Times*, July 17, 1980.
96. Quoted in *Sports Illustrated*, July 16, 1984.
97. Quoted in *Los Angeles Times*, February 2, 1983.
98. Quoted in *Los Angeles Times*, April 27, 1982.
99. See, for example, *Los Angeles Times*, April 27, 1982; June 28, 1982; October 12, 1982; December 12, 1982.
100. *Los Angeles Times*, May 20, 1982.
101. See, for example, *Los Angeles Times*, July 21, 1983.
102. *Los Angeles Times*, May 14, 1984.
103. Quoted in *Los Angeles Times*, November 3, 1983.
104. Quoted in *Los Angeles Times*, May 12, 1984. See also *Los Angeles Times*, April 8, 1984.
105. *Los Angeles Times*, April 15, 1984.
106. Quoted in *Los Angeles Times*, May 15, 1984.
107. Quoted in *Los Angeles Times*, July 24, 1984.
108. *Los Angeles Times*, August 7, 1984.
109. *Los Angeles Times*, June 27, 1984, and elsewhere. Iran, primarily concerned with its revolution and the war with Iraq, stayed away from Moscow as well as Los Angeles. Albania has not attended the Games for many years. Libya pulled out on the eve of the Olympics when the U.S. State Department denied visas to three Libyan journalists, alleging they were not reporters but terrorists.
110. *Los Angeles Times*, July 28, 1985.
111. *Los Angeles Times*, July 26, 1984. A perceptive view of Romanian domestic and foreign policy is presented by Irene and Raymond Vianu in that issue.
112. *Los Angeles Times*, July 31, 1984.
113. *Los Angeles Times*, July 29, 1984.
114. *Los Angeles Times*, August 13, 1984.
115. See pp. 25-26 and especially note 61 in Chapter Two.
116. See p. 26.

117. *Sports Illustrated*, August 3, 1981; *Los Angeles Times*, September 22, 1981.

118. *Sports Illustrated*, August 3, 1981.

119. *Sports Illustrated*, April 9, 1984.

120. *San Francisco Examiner*, March 17, 1985.

121. *Los Angeles Times*, July 23, 1984.

122. *Los Angeles Times*, June 24, 1984.

123. Espy, p. 182.

124. Quoted in Espy, p. 182.

125. Edwards (1985).

126. Espy, p. 178.

127. Espy, pp. 179-182.

128. This definition of success boils down to winning. Since U.S. society focuses on winning, so do its advertisements. Thus, these ads are discussed for purposes of illustration, not criticism. See p. 7.

129. *Sports Illustrated*, February 14, 1983.

130. *Los Angeles Times*, September 26, 1983.

131. Quoted in *Los Angeles Times*, August 2, 1985.

132. Quoted in *Sports Illustrated*, August 13, 1984. Emphasis in original.

133. I do not know who manufactured these buttons. My parents bought one.

134. USOC, p. 5. The writer is USOC Director of Communications Mike Moran.

135. LAOOC (1984d), pp. 33-34. The specter of the "capitalist Olympics" was present on the other side of the card, which read "Enjoy Coca-Cola." (Coca-Cola, not the LAOOC, included the card in the program.)

136. *Los Angeles Times*, August 13, 1984.

137. *Los Angeles Times*, August 2, 1984.

138. *Los Angeles Times*, August 13, 1984.

139. *Los Angeles Times*, August 2, 1985.

140. See pp. 29-30 for a discussion of post-World War II Germany and the Olympic movement.

141. Espy, pp. 36-37.

142. Quoted in Guttmann, p. 146. The excerpt comes from a letter written by IOC member Tung Shou-yi.

143. Guttmann, pp. 142-147.

144. Press Commission of the COC (1984a), p. 5.

145. Guttmann, pp. 147-150.

146. Kanin, p. 75.

147. Espy, pp. 183-185; Kanin, p. 110.

148. The 1976 situation is explained further on p. 30.

149. Espy, p. 183.

150. Press Commission of the COC (1984a), p. 5.

151. *Los Angeles Times*, March 23, 1979.

152. *Los Angeles Times*, November 27, 1979.

153. Espy, pp. 187-188.

154. *Los Angeles Times*, August 3, 1980.

155. *Los Angeles Times*, March 24, 1981.

156. Press Commission of the COC (1984a), p. 7.

157. Quoted in *Los Angeles Times*, August 14, 1984. The newspaper is *Neue Kronen Zeitung*.

158. *Los Angeles Times*, July 30, 1984. Also see pp. 38-42.

159. The 1976 Montreal Games did not have any security or traffic problems, and all of the world's major sports powers were there. But Montreal's legacy is that of a billion-dollar deficit.

160. *Los Angeles Times*, July 31, 1985. LAOOC volunteers did end up receiving box lunches during the Games.

161. Quoted in *Los Angeles Times*, April 8, 1984.

162. *Los Angeles Times*, July 31, 1985.

163. *Los Angeles Times*, September 12, 1984.

164. *Los Angeles Times*, July 31, 1985.

165. Quoted in *Los Angeles Times*, July 31, 1985. The speaker is Henry Durand, a vice-president of Loyola Marymount University. He coordinated relations between the university, which hosted weightlifting events in the 1984 Games, and the LAOOC. "I think that is obscene," said Durand, "because we had to fight for every penny we got."

166. Quoted in *Los Angeles Times*, November 1, 1984. The speaker is unnamed.

167. *Los Angeles Times*, November 23, 1984.

168. *Los Angeles Times*, October 3, 1984.

169. *Los Angeles Times*, September 27, 1984; September 28, 1984; October 3, 1984.

170. *Los Angeles Times*, December 20, 1984. In fact, when the LAOOC officially dissolved in February 1986, the surplus pool had reached $235 million (*Los Angeles Times*, February 5, 1986)

171. Quoted in *Los Angeles Times*, November 10, 1984.

172. *Los Angeles Times*, November 10, 1984; December 3, 1984.

173. LAOOC alumni organization newsletter.

174. *Los Angeles Times*, December 3, 1984.

175. *Los Angeles Times*, November 11, 1984.

176. *Los Angeles Times*, February 11, 1985.

177. In March 1986, the USOC reluctantly reversed its position and allocated $1 million of its share of the surplus to partially reimburse NOCs for their expenses. (*Los Angeles Times*, March 28, 1986) The surplus has now been divided according to the conditions in the 1978 contract: 20 percent to national sports federations in the United States, 40 percent to the USOC, and 40 percent to the promotion of amateur sport in southern California, the last administered by the newly created LAOOC Amateur Athletics Foundation.

178. *Los Angeles Times*, December 30, 1984.

Chapter Four
WHITHER THE OLYMPICS?

The Olympics are war without shooting.
George Orwell

The Olympic Games have long been a troubled institution. In part, the sickness is self-inflicted. Coubertin founded the Games on idealistic principles, and the IOC has so preoccupied itself with perpetuating those tenets that it has become almost oblivious to contemporary conditions. Columnist William Buckley calls the Olympics "obnoxious, a bombastic rhetoric of idealism not only unrelated to reality, but assiduously flouted."[1] But the illness also has external causes. While politics is not the only culprit, Chapters Two and Three have demonstrated that the blend of politics and the Olympics is seldom smooth. After the Soviet Union announced its 1984 boycott, some observers thought the mix had grown toxic. Olga Connolly, who won the gold medal in the discus in the 1956 Melbourne Games, termed the Soviet boycott a "death blow."[2] IOC member James Worrall, himself a former Olympian, said, "This certainly brings us pretty damn close to the end."[3] The *London Daily Express* opined, "Better that the whole rotten mess be interred as quickly as possible. It has been a terminal case for years."[4] In the wake of the Los Angeles Games, the Olympics appear to be afflicted with chronic but not fatal problems. Let us focus on the political difficulties and then ask: whither the Olympics?

The 1984 Games, said a Swiss newspaper, meant "enthusiasm wherever you looked. Los Angeles gave the world super Games, a sports festival the like of which has not been seen for a long time and one that was urgently needed to assure the survival of the Olympic movement."[5] Perhaps

the most important legacy Los Angeles left was the huge
surplus. Although it engendered some ill will within the
LAOOC and around the world, as discussed in Chapter Three,
the substantial profit proved that a deficit need not
necessarily accompany a well-run Games. The Los Angeles
experience demonstrated that profit as well as prestige can
accrue to an Olympic host, an enticing combination to
cities around the world.[6] As a result, the IOC is not
likely to encounter a repeat of the 1977 situation, when
Los Angeles's bid for the 1984 Games was unopposed, anytime
soon. Nine cities displayed serious interest in staging the
1992 Games; and Paris, Brisbane, Belgrade, Amsterdam,
Barcelona, and Birmingham (England) all made formal bids.
In October 1986, the IOC awarded the 1992 Games to
Samaranch's hometown of Barcelona.[7] The 1996 Games are
likely to be held in Athens, celebrating the centennial of
the revival of the Olympics. The People's Republic of China
has talked seriously of hosting the 2000 Games.[8] Flushed
with the success of the 1984 Games, the private Southern
California Committee for the Olympic Games reestablished
itself and has begun lobbying for the Olympics to return to
Los Angeles in 2004.[9]

Interest in the Games is healthy, even if the Games
themselves are not. A prime objective in Los Angeles's
spartan bid to host the Games, said Mayor Tom Bradley, was
"to avoid incurring the deficits which have plagued recent
Olympic Games. We are convinced that, unless this trend is
halted, the future of the Olympics is very much in
jeopardy."[10] Even the IOC, as responsible as any host city
for the increasing extravagance of pre-1984 Games, rallied
behind the only city willing to host the 1984 Olympics. A
letter signed by Samaranch and Executive Director Monique
Berlioux read in part: "The Games will be organized with an
original concept and we have no doubts of their successful
outcome. This outcome is very important for future Games.
The International Olympic Committee fully supports the
LAOOC."[11] Yet the evidence indicates that neither the IOC
nor the 1988 host city, Seoul, South Korea, has any
interest in following Los Angeles's example.

South Korea and its capital, Seoul, were ravaged in
the Korean War. Three decades later, the nation and the
city have made an extraordinary economic and physical
recovery. Seoul residents call their home the "Phoenix City
of the Orient,"[12] and from the ashes of the war has arisen
a metropolis as modern as any in the world, complete with
"high-rise banks and office buildings, luxurious Western-
style hotels, good public transportation--and choking
traffic."[13] South Korea is eager to show off this
development to a world that, the Koreans feel, has for too
long overlooked their country and discussed Asian economy
and culture solely in terms of China and Japan. "Koreans
have a driving need to prove something to the world," says

author Joungwon Kim. "The 1988 Olympics is Korea's chance to show ourselves to the world and say, 'Look, we too have greatness in us.'"[14] In order for the world to believe that, the Korean people have to believe it, and former Seoul Olympic Organizing Committee (SLOOC) President Lee Yong Ho sees the Games as the perfect vehicle for fostering that pride. "This is an occasion," says Lee, "to prove ourselves to the world and, more important, to ourselves."[15] Clearly, the 1988 Games will emphasize showcasing the host nation as much as any previous Olympics.[16]

The South Korean government, the primary patron of the goals of national pride and global admiration through the Olympics, is closely tied to the staging of the 1988 Games. Indeed, Lee, the former SLOOC president, is South Korea's minister of sport.[17] Park Seh Jik, the current SLOOC chief, assumed that post after serving as deputy director of the country's national intelligence agency.[18] In order to best show off South Korea to the world, the government is sacrificing economy for extravagance and is, in fact, paying much of the SLOOC's costs--about 50 percent of the expected 1988 expenditures.[19] As journalist Kenneth Reich notes, "There is every indication that the IOC likes it that way."[20] So much, at least for now, for the Los Angeles example.

U.S. television networks have given the SLOOC a headache. The local organizers counted on the sale of U.S. broadcast rights to provide the second largest share of revenues--over 15 percent--in the 1988 budget. With ABC having paid $225 million to broadcast the Los Angeles Games and $309 million for the 1988 Winter Games in Calgary, Canada, the SLOOC expected that at least one of the three U.S. commercial networks would make a $600 million bid.[21] None did, and the agreement Seoul organizers and NBC reached is worth between $300 and 500 million to the SLOOC, depending on the network's level of profits.[22] The reluctance of American television to meet Seoul's asking price may, some officials say, doom the 1988 Games to a deficit.[23] The sizable deficit from the 1976 Montreal Games still has financial and political ramifications in Canada, and any similarly large loss in Seoul could be perilous to South Korea's young and fragile democracy.

A huge deficit would almost surely accompany a boycott of the 1988 Olympics. In the event of a boycott or other major disturbance, the SLOOC might very well have to refund much, if not all, of NBC's money.[24] If Seoul might take a loss even with NBC's complete payment, return of those funds would make a deficit a virtual certainty. It is by no means clear that a boycott will not affect the 1988 Games. The analysis in Chapter Three shows that the Soviet decision to boycott the Los Angeles Olympics was primarily motivated by U.S. leadership of the movement to stay away from the 1980 Moscow Games. The Soviets have no such need to take revenge upon South Korea, and it is reasonable to think that one of the world's major sports powers would not pass up the world's premier athletic festival twice in a row. But, despite Moscow's pledges to attend the Seoul Games, several arguments call those premises into question. The Soviet Union does not recognize South Korea, and neither do Russia's allies. For that matter, neither do many black African nations and the People's Republic of China, none of whom are strangers to Olympic politics. In all, 37 IOC member nations do not maintain diplomatic relations with South Korea.[25] Unofficial diplomatic contacts between Moscow and Seoul have been strained since the Soviets shot down a Korean Air Lines plane in September 1983, killing 269 people.[26] Harry Edwards, who correctly predicted the 1984 Soviet boycott, says he would be "surprised" to see Russian athletes in Seoul.[27]

South Korea need not look all the way to Moscow for potential 1988 political problems. Just 25 miles from the center of Seoul's sports complex lies a demilitarized zone, the territory beyond which belongs to North Korea.[28] While the Korean people largely hope for eventual reunification, the governments of North and South Korea are bitter foes. North Korea refuses to watch idly as its southern rival scores political prestige points through its Seoul showcase.[29] Hoping for part of the global attention, North Korea has insisted that the IOC allow, and that South Korea agree to, North Korea's co-hosting the 1988 Games.[30]

At first, South Korea resisted. The government and the SLOOC--effectively partners in producing the 1988 Games--understandably objected to North Korea's demand. After all, they had spent hundreds of thousands of dollars to win the 1988 Games and hundreds of millions more to build the facilities necessary to stage them. As discussed above, the Seoul government was just as interested in showing off its country as it was in showing off the world's finest athletes. The IOC had given South Korea the Olympic platform the government so desperately wanted, and Seoul worried that, just as the IOC had given, so the IOC would take away.

With the memories of Los Angeles and Moscow fresh in its collective mind, the IOC approached the North Korean question from a different angle. The IOC made clear as early as 1984 that the 1988 Games would not be moved, acknowledging the enormous amount of resources Seoul had invested and affirming the IOC's tradition of bringing the Olympics to new places around the globe.[31] Yet the very fact that the IOC felt compelled to issue such a statement was a tacit admission of North Korea's political clout. The overwhelming majority of countries that do not recognize South Korea are allies of North Korea, and Cuba and Ethiopia have already declared that they will boycott the

Seoul Games if North Korea has not reached a satisfactory accord with the IOC and South Korea.[32] Considering his position as IOC president, Samaranch made an unusual if understated concession in July 1986. "We have encountered a number of political problems in the last few years," he acknowledged. "They may not disappear by the year 1988."[33]

Desperate for a boycott-free Olympiad, the IOC steered South Korea off the road of intransigence and onto the avenue of compromise. After protracted negotiations, the IOC formally offered North Korea the opportunity to host all of the archery and table tennis competitions, a cycling road race, preliminary soccer matches, and a share of the cultural events surrounding the sporting festival.[34] North Korea accepted that proposal but has continued to wrangle for full "co-host" status and, accordingly, more events. North Korean Olympic Committee President Kim Yu Sun has called the IOC offer "too small," and he has threatened a boycott if the IOC and South Korea do not present a more generous proposal.[35]

It is difficult to accurately gauge the degree to which Pyongyang may be bluffing. Then again, it is difficult to accurately gauge anything of substance happening inside North Korea. The nation controls its borders as rigidly as any country in the world. North Korea accepts only several hundred Western visitors each year, and airlines link North Korea with just three foreign cities.[36] If North Korea co-hosts--in any form--the 1988 Games, the IOC will require that Pyongyang welcome a group of athletes, officials, journalists, and other foreigners that will number well into the thousands and that will represent countries from around the world. As SLOOC Secretary-General Lee Ha Woo observes, "That is the big question. If they accept foreigners into their country, it's going to be a major departure from their policies."[37]

Pyongyang insists it is ready to satisfy the IOC's concerns. In fact, North Korea has erected two stadia--one seating 150,000 people--a smaller athletic complex, and a press center as proof of its determination to share the Olympic stage.[38] Whether the IOC--and Seoul officials--can satisfy Pyongyang's concerns remains very much an open question. If the IOC and the two countries cannot reach some sort of agreement, North Korea may well seek the spotlight anyway, and South Korea will become the loser. Neither a terrorist incident nor the oppressive security needed to prevent such an attack from barely more than 25 miles away will give the world the positive impression of South Korea that the Seoul Games are so pointedly designed to convey.[39]

Politically, South Korea might be a culprit as well as a victim. Seoul is eager to display to a watching world South Korean advances in economic, cultural, and political spheres. However, an increasingly unified opposition is

rapidly gathering public support and challenging the
government's definition of political progress--challenging,
in fact, the government's key concepts of South Korean
politics. These dissidents threaten to occupy a stage--with
a bright spotlight--during the 1988 Games.

Popular support has not been a hallmark of recent
South Korean regimes. Park Chung Hee used military backing
to fill a power vacuum in 1972, usurping the South Korean
presidency and ruling with an iron fist until 1979, when he
was assassinated. Again a power vacuum formed, and again
the country's armed forces played a key role in anointing a
leader. The new president, Chun Doo Hwan, took over after
several months of turmoil and promptly extended the period
of domestic turbulence by issuing a declaration that
prolonged martial law. On the day following Chun's edict,
189 people were killed in a riot in Kwangju, a provincial
capital 175 miles south of Seoul.[40]

Spurred by the United States, Chun has made overtures
toward democracy. South Korea adopted a Western-style but
Chun-flavored constitution that limits the president to a
single, seven-year term. Accordingly, Chun has pledged to
leave office when his term expires in March 1988. In
addition, in a 1985 deal apparently brokered in Washington,
Chun permitted leading dissident Kim Dae Jung to return to
South Korea from exile in the United States.[41] But Chun has
been less than comfortable with a traditional offshoot of a
democratic system, political protest.

Although Chun barred Kim from joining a political
party as a condition of his return, it is hardly
coincidental that anti-government rallies multiplied
following his homecoming. A massive demonstration
commemorating the fifth anniversary of the Kwangju riot
attracted 5,000 to Kwangju itself and thousands more to
simultaneous gatherings throughout the country.[42] Seven
thousand people rallied in Seoul in March 1986.[43] Two weeks
later, 20,000 assembled in Pusan.[44] A crowd of 60,000
protested in Kwangju the following week.[45] In October 1986,
more than 3,000 students occupied 5 buildings at Kunkook
University in Seoul for several days.[46] A correspondent
reported "nearly daily anti-Chun demonstrations on the
nation's campuses."[47]

Chun has not been tolerant of the wave of dissent.
Police wielding tear gas have broken up numerous rallies.
Chun has ordered mass arrests on a scale unseen since the
1980 riots that surrounded his consolidation of power.[48]
The National Council of Churches estimated in May 1986 that
South Korea's jails held 1015 political prisoners, a number
opposition leaders claimed was 600 too low.[49] Chun placed
Kim under house arrest virtually any time the opposition
held a meeting or staged a rally, including 20 separate
detentions from February through July 1986, using upwards
of 1,000 police at times to keep the 60-year-old Kim inside

his house.[50] The human rights group Asia Watch cites South Korea for rights violations in clamping down on dissidents and student and labor activists.[51]

Despite the repression, the singularity and persistence of the opposition and its goal achieved modest success. Kim Dae Jung and Kim Young Sam, two loud and usually divergent opposition voices, joined in chorus, forming the Committee for the Promotion of Democracy (CPD)--a citizens' group that skirts Chun's ban on Kim Dae Jung's association with a political party--and supporting an allied party, the New Korea Democratic Party (NKDP).[52] This unified opposition cultivated a large and growing popular following by focusing its efforts on once easily comprehensible objective: direct presidential elections. The current Chun constitution calls for an electoral college composed of 5,500 delegates to choose the president, a system the CPD and its supporters argue is open to fraud because Chun's Democratic Justice Party (DJP) controls South Korea's National Assembly.[53] A 1986 poll found that more than 70 percent of South Koreans wanted direct presidential elections, an amazing testament to the effectiveness of the opposition campaign when one considers that the government conducted the survey and that the government controls the nation's media. As reporter Sam Jameson observed, "Many [South] Koreans simply do not believe that Chun's military-backed regime would allow for fair elections."[54]

Chun slowly moderated his intransigence. In February 1986, he responded in typical fashion to the start of a petition drive calling for direct presidential elections by seizing signed petitions, raiding CPD and NKDP headquarters, and placing Kim Dae Jung under house arrest for 11 days.[55] In the months that followed, however, Chun consented to meet with opposition leaders--but not with either Kim--and pledged to abide by any constitutional changes approved by the National Assembly, even though he reiterated that he saw no need for such reform.[56] Then, in a surprise announcement, Chun's DJP and the opposition NKDP agreed to form a joint National Assembly committee for constitutional reform.[57] Three convergent factors accounted for Chun's softening his public stance: pressure from Washington, pressure from growing opposition from within South Korea, and the fall of Ferdinand Marcos in February 1986. CPD and NKDP leaders wasted no time in comparing the fall of a U.S.-backed authoritarian ruler in the Philippines with what they considered a virtually identical situation in South Korea. "I hope Chun will not be a second Marcos," remarked Kim Young Sam, "[but] if he keeps turning a deaf ear to the demand for democracy, he will have to flee the country."[58] Kim Dae Jung commented, "President Reagan may be a conservative, but he is a pragmatist, too. America could not help supporting the majority in the

Philippines. For the sake of U.S. self-interest, Reagan cannot help supporting democracy in foreign countries."[59] Kim Dae Jung sounded convinced that the "people power" Corazon Aquino mobilized to topple Marcos in a relatively bloodless revolution could be duplicated in South Korea:

> Chun will have to choose whether to fight the people to the end and create his own misfortune, or to choose a direct presidential form of democracy and a peaceful transfer of power desired by the people. The people will not tolerate dictatorship any more.[60]

Chun hopes that South Koreans will view 1988 as a year to celebrate the Olympics, not "tolerate [a] dictatorship." He has repeatedly stated that he would be amenable to constitutional reform after the Seoul Games, in part because he would presumably be out of office by then but primarily because he sincerely believes South Koreans should join together for the Olympics rather than split in political battles. In the words of SLOOC Secretary-General Lee Ha Woo, "In South Korea, it is the hope . . . that the entire country will grow together, with the Olympics taking us forward. The Games become a total national endeavor, a national state of mind."[61] As discussed earlier, Chun and SLOOC officials feel the 1988 Olympics will serve to legitimize South Korea in the eyes of the world. But not all of his countrymen agree that unity for the Olympics—indeed, the Olympics itself—is an undisputable top priority. Says Seoul Cardinal Stephen Kim, "If one agrees that the constitution has to be revised, why wait to revise it? Why not change it as soon as possible?"[62] Even more direct was Kim Dae Jung's impassioned appeal to a crowded rally. "Are the Olympics more important than democracy?" he asked. "Is there any event that can be more important than democracy?"[63]

"No" continues to be the answer from opposition quarters. Talks between the DJP and the NKDP in the National Assembly stalled, and the frustrated Kims broke from the NKDP to defy Chun and form their own hard-line opposition party, the Reunification Democratic Party (RDP). An enraged Chun responded by cancelling all discussion of constitutional reform until after the 1988 Games.[64] With the avenue of negotiation turning into a dead end, dissidents renewed their calls for popular support of their cause. Opposition sparks flew, but, ironically, Chun himself ignited the widespread fire the Kims and their colleagues had worked so long to build.

On June 10, 1987, Chun named Roh Tae Woo as the DJP's presidential candidate. With Chun's ruling party in control of the National Assembly, the RDP saw an electoral college system that practically guaranteed that Roh would succeed his military academy classmate and longtime mentor as South Korea's president. Thus, in the span of two months, Chun had broken off all talks with opposition leaders and virtually anointed a successor. Dissidents no longer held a faint hope of waiting out Chun, for they feared political reform would rank no higher on the agenda of a Roh presidency.

Chun's proclamation provoked the popular uprising that the Kims, for all their efforts, could not. Over the next 17 days, violent protest swept South Korea with a ferocity never before seen during Chun's reign. Demonstrators rallied daily, chanting for change and hurling rocks and bombs at police that fired more than 350,000 canisters of tear gas and detained more than 17,000 people.[65] The government's show of force did not deter increasing numbers of protestors from returning, almost by ritual, to battle-weary areas of Seoul and dozens of other cities where the pervasive stench of tear gas lingered from one day's rally to the next.

The "who" and "where" of the June protests foretold their eventual success. Throughout the Chun years, while anti-government demonstrations flourished on the country's college campuses, the rest of South Korea looked upon its youth with detachment. Personal and national economic concerns, especially in light of South Korea's rise in the standard of living and rise to world prominence, outweighed political affairs. But, in the days after June 10, the protests spilled outside the universities and onto the streets. Church officials and some business leaders took the students' side for the first time, arguing that Roh's unchallenged succession might indefinitely prolong Chun's unwritten policy that economic strength outweighed political liberties. The middle class, secure in that economic strength, at last joined in the demonstrations, and worldwide television cameras followed. The South Korean "people power" that Kim Dae Jung had hoped would grow had truly blossomed.[66]

As rioting rocked South Korea, Chun grew increasingly stubborn and increasingly isolated. While Chun typically painted student protestors as radicals and Communist sympathizers, the growing revolt reflected the participation of segments of South Korean society too broad to wear such labels. The outside world recognized this, through nightly television footage of the daily unrest. The IOC recognized this, bravely proclaiming that nothing short of civil war would move the 1988 Games but privately fearing that very prospect. The United States recognized this, counseling Chun not to declare martial law or deploy the military against the South Korean people. Even the country's military--without which Chun and every previous South Korean leader would not have come to power--

recognized this. "The military is keenly aware," said a Seoul political editor, "that the birth of another leader with guns and swords will not receive the support of the public."[67] In the end, Roh recognized what Chun would not.

On June 29, just after 9 a.m., Roh took to the airwaves of the state-run South Korean television network, normally off the air during the day. In a 17-minute address, Chun's longtime ally and handpicked successor recommended the adoption of direct presidential elections, the goal for which the opposition fought so fiercely and against which Chun battled with equal resolve. With nearly three weeks worth of recurring and violent protest gripping the country, observers expected Roh to offer a compromise in an attempt to quell the turmoil in the streets. On this day, however, Roh would bid for a page in the history books, not just a seat at a negotiation table. Roh stunned friends and enemies of his ruling DJP by acceding to virtually every demand on what opposition leaders conceded was a wish list for political discussion. Roh's proposals, in addition to direct presidential elections, included the restoration of Kim Dae Jung's full civil rights, release of all but the most violent political prisoners, and increased freedoms for the press and opposition political parties. In a dramatic conclusion to an already extraordinary speech, Roh vowed to resign as the DJP's presidential candidate if Chun did not approve the reform package.[68]

So ended South Korea's bloodless revolution. Opposition leaders graciously praised Roh while declaring victory. "Roh's statement covered our most important demands," said Kim Young Sam. "This was the people's victory. We should give all credit to the people."[69] While Roh's surprise speech and threatened resignation all but forced Chun to endorse the reforms he had long opposed, adoption of Roh's proposals did offer Chun an opportunity to realize his dream of becoming the first South Korean president to leave office peacefully. "I clearly recognize . . . the general public has an ardent desire to choose the president directly," conceded Chun. "Let us work another miracle by developing Korea into a model of political development deserving to be so recorded in world history. We must not be content with having merely become a model of economic development."[70] Roh, the architect of reform, modestly depicted himself as a public servant. "The people are the masters of the country," he said, "and the people's will must come before everything else."[71] Roh left it to political observers to point out that he had transformed himself into a champion of the people and, in the free and direct presidential election he promised, a suddenly popular candidate somewhat distanced from Chun.

Both sides cited a need for South Korea to repair its image before the 1988 Games. "With only a short time left before the Olympics," Roh told the nation, "all of us share a responsibility to avoid national humiliation."[72] The country's substantial financial and emotional investment in the 1988 Games did not escape Kim Young Sam's attention, either. "Once President Chun accepts the [Roh] proposals and we have a new government in power," said Kim, "then we won't have any more problems, and we won't have any more demonstrations. We will, I'm sure, have a successful Olympic Games."[73]

But the promise of democracy, as Kim hints, hardly guarantees the realization of democracy. While Chun did indeed ratify the Roh reforms, their implementation has been slow. The government has released a modest number of political prisoners, but compromise is an unfamiliar art in South Korean politics and, two months after Roh's dramatic address, negotiations on consitutional revision and the mechanisms of electoral change continued without agreement. Fearing that the excitement surrounding Roh's speech might mask a dearth of substantive reform, students started a new round of demonstrations on college campuses. On August 25, South Korean police arrested several student activists--the first such detentions since Roh announced his reforms--and thus hardened the skepticism brewing among many opposition leaders.[74]

The Seoul Games begin in September 1988, and political tension in South Korea may boil just as the world turns its attention to Seoul and its final preparation for the Olympics. Within weeks of the 1988 Winter Games--when the media begin to preview the Summer Games--Chun is scheduled to leave office. South Korea has never witnessed a peaceful transfer of power. Chun could not have assumed the presidency without the backing of the nation's military, and it is entirely possible that the armed forces, despite their June 1987 silence, will play a critical role in South Korean politics in 1988--whether Chun steps down or not. Neither scenario--Chun remaining in office against the popular will and his own promises, or Chun leaving amid a battle for the presidency--presents a tranquil picture.

In addition, Chun is not the only one who realizes that the Seoul Games will show off South Korea to the world. South Korean students protested during the 1986 Asian Games, an event SLOOC officials considered a dress rehearsal for the 1988 Olympics. Despite renewed student demonstrations in the country, SLOOC President Park Seh Jik sounds confident they will cease during the Games. "I think the students are coming to be aware of how important the Olympics are and how unwise it is to behave that way in a critical period," says Park with optimism reminiscent of Avery Brundage.[75] Of course, Park is correct when he says that students understand the importance of the Olympics, but it is for that very reason that they figure to take advantage of this global stage to amplify their dissent. At the Asian Games--as well as at most recent rallies--South

Korean riot police armed with tear gas have dispersed opposition protests. Widespread demonstrations--such as those surrounding the 1968 Mexico City Games--would indeed reach a worldwide audience and, whether broken up or not, would make the goal of showcasing South Korean progress ring hollow.

Still more political issues could haunt the 1988 Games. South Africa, itching to participate in the Olympics, has applied to the IOC for readmission into the Olympic family and seeks to send a national team to Seoul.[76] The Palestine Liberation Organization (PLO) has talked seriously of petitioning for IOC recognition and competing in future Olympiads.[77] Consideration of either request will concentrate almost exclusively on political factors, and Samaranch will need to employ all of his diplomatic skill to keep South African and PLO issues from opening a wide rift among the IOC membership. Of course, the outline above does not preclude other global political occurrences that could have a major impact on the 1988 Games. After all, the Soviet Union did not invade Afghanistan until six months before the 1980 Moscow Games.

Despite the success at Los Angeles, then, all is not blissful within the Olympic movement. If any good came out of the boycotts of 1976, 1980, and 1984, it should have been in the direction of reform. The Games have evolved into a major political as well as sporting event, and the only party that can alter that trend is the IOC, whose charter members built a structure predisposed toward political uses. The IOC, however, has shown little inclination to change. In the wake of the third straight Olympiad disrupted by boycotts, the last two with a superpower leading the way, the IOC called a meeting for December 1984 to discuss possible action. Even though the session is billed as an "emergency" one, no sense of urgency prevailed and no meaningful reform resulted. Boycott sanctions, the IOC decided, would be limited to refusal to accredit NOC officials from countries not participating in a particular Games. The IOC did not even consider other pressing issues, among them controversies regarding amateurism and drug use clearly worthy of its "emergency" agenda.[78] "We in the IOC can do many things, but what we cannot do is rule the world," Samaranch responded to critics charging his organization with inaction. "The last two boycotts, of Moscow and Los Angeles, were due to political reasons and only to political reasons."[79]

Samaranch is correct, but the impetus for altering the political environment that spawns boycotts must lie with the IOC. That body has not--and will not, in the foreseeable future--act decisively to change the Olympic format. Samaranch acknowledges the result:

To boycott the Olympic Games has become
extremely spectacular. The rulers doing so
know it very well. They secure, for months on
end and with little risk, the headlines of
all the information media. They capture world
attention. The Games are a formidable sound
box.[80]

Samaranch's last sentence is the most important; after all,
the 1980 boycott did not prompt the Soviet Union to
withdraw its troops from Afghanistan. But, while there is
"little risk" of an Olympic boycott effecting political
change, there is also "little risk" of the IOC taking any
measurable action to discourage countries from using the
Games as a "formidable sound box."

The history and composition of the IOC do not lend
themselves to optimism about the future of the Olympics.
One of Coubertin's primary precepts in founding the IOC was
that its members be chosen by the IOC and not be appointed
by constituent countries. National representatives are thus
ambassadors of the IOC to their homelands and not vice
versa. The IOC is fiercely proud and protective of its
independence, and relations with NOCs and sports
federations are conducted on the basis of unyielding IOC
authority over the Olympic Games. This doctrine takes
precedence over the good of the Games in Olympic affairs.
In 1981, for example, the IOC held a rare International
Athletic Congress, bringing together representatives of the
IOC, NOCs, sports federations, athletes, the media, and
even UNESCO.[81] Despite the apparent wealth of Olympic
knowledge present at the Congress, the IOC, concerned more
with self-preservation than with improving the Games,
structured the meeting to allow for discussion but not
decision making. Kenneth Reich wrote: "The format of the
Congress has been set up in such a way as to dilute the
force of any reform movement that may surface . . . from
outside the IOC."[82]

It is difficult to envision any drive for reform
originating within the IOC. Despite Coubertin's grand plan
for IOC members' autonomy, delegates from Eastern bloc
nations represent the views of their governments just as
well as they would in any other world forum, including the
United Nations. Since Western members generally do not
directly represent their governments, these delegates are
often wealthy, conservative, and older gentlemen who have
the time and money to travel around the world attending IOC
meetings--the same type of people who have run and shaped
the Olympics since their revival.[83] Although Samaranch's
realistic talk is a welcome relief from the pious rhetoric
often emanating from the IOC presidency, the body itself
remains idealistic and reactionary. The IOC did not admit
women to its membership until 1981. It continually objects

to memorializing the 11 Israeli Olympians killed at the 1972 Munich Games, claiming, in all seriousness, that doing so would politicize the Olympic Games.[84] Even the athletes can only advise the IOC, despite the fact that, as Edwards puts it, "Nobody is going to come to see the International Olympic Committee run the 100 meters."[85] He remarks that it is "impossible to force the IOC to do anything."[86]

Bearing in mind the IOC's behavior, let us discuss several commonly made proposals for reducing the magnitude of politics inherent in the Olympics. Many of these plans view nationalism as the chief political component of the Games, and the recommendations thus focus on the nationalistic trappings of the Olympics. The suggestions, many of which will appear familiar to readers, include curtailing or eliminating the raising of national flags and playing of national anthems during victory ceremonies, abolishing national uniforms, allowing athletes only to march behind the Olympic flag and to the Olympic hymn, and structuring the Games so that competitors are not associated with their country.

That last concept was tried at the 1981 IAAF World Cup, a world-class track and field meet.[87] Officials divided athletes into nine teams: four national squads--the United States, the Soviet Union, East Germany, and host Italy--and five regional squads representing Europe, Africa, Asia, Oceania, and the Americas. In addition to attempting to defuse nationalistic elements, the idea allowed for much more balanced competition, as the participants from weaker countries pooled their talent to better challenge the athletes from the world's major sports powers. However, despite the regional framework, fans, rivals, and the media associated competitors with countries, not continents. Accounts of the men's 100-meter dash, for instance, reported that Great Britain's Allen Wells edged Ghana's Ernest Obeng for the victory. One did not read that Europe's Wells defeated Africa's Obeng.[88]

This type of competition might have been feasible as a method of reducing nationalism many years ago. With the advent of instant worldwide communication, though, the tendency of the media to simplify stories has been amplified. Since identifying athletes by country has traditionally been the easiest way of reporting, it will continue to be done in that manner, even if the IOC were to request a change in the style of coverage. After all, it was the media and not the IOC that instituted point totals and medal counts for each nation, a now familiar and virtually mandatory part of Olympic coverage--and how much simpler can reporting get? Besides, it is highly unlikely that the conservative IOC will adopt any type of measure at variance with long-standing Olympic customs, regardless of how inappropriate or potentially harmful those customs may be. In 1980, for instance, organizers of the Lake Placid

Winter Games suggested that, in the opening ceremonies, the competitors march in behind their national flags but march out under the Olympic banner. Reich explains the IOC's unsurprising refusal of this very minor change:

> There was nothing in the Lake Placid proposal that would have changed the victory ceremonies, where the medals are awarded. National flags would still have been raised over the winners and the national anthem of the gold medalist would have been played.
>
> But, with scarcely a serious look at the proposal, the IOC . . . rejected it, saying it would be contrary to tradition.[89]

Creating a permanent site for the Games has become a popular recommendation. Since the 1980 and 1984 boycotts were primarily directed at the host countries, advocates of this reform contend that this sort of protest would end if a satisfactory permanent host is selected. Even under the assumption that this hypothesis is valid, the task of finding a suitable site would be a formidable one. The original home of the Olympics, Greece, is the favorite of many proponents of this alternative. But that country is far from neutral today. Many IOC members might consider contemporary Greece's political instability, poor relations with Turkey, and spotty human rights record as causes for concern with--if not outright objection to--the choice of Greece as the permanent Olympic Games site.[90]

A 1981 IOC report, while not making a binding recommendation, cast doubt on the Greece option. In addition to the distinctly political considerations, the report cited other factors that do not place Greece in a positive light. The country's summer weather is oppressively hot. Holding the Games there permanently would severely strain the nation's infrastructure. Ironically, construction of Olympic facilities in Greece might involve tearing down some treasured sites of the ancient Games.[91] If Greece is not a viable alternative, proponents say, then politically neutral Switzerland is. While no country would likely gain greater world approval, the question of cost remains. It is doubtful that Switzerland or any other nation could bear the considerable financial burden of staging the Olympics every four years. The IOC could surmount that obstacle by assessing a fee to each member country, but the disappointing experience of the United Nations in collecting contributions from its assembly makes this proposition appear infeasible.[92] In any case, an IOC so protective of its fiefdom is highly unlikely to surrender what has become its premier duty and privilege, that of selecting Olympic hosts.

According to another suggestion, if the Games continue

to be held at rotating sites, the IOC should go one step further and split the events of a particular Olympiad among a small group of cities in various countries. Politically, the primary virtue of this alternative would be to defuse the potential for boycotts aimed at host nations, since there would no longer be a single host. Let us again proceed on the assumption that the theory is true. The Games' reputation as the premier international sporting event is due largely to their scale. The grandeur of the Olympics, for both athletic and political participants, has come to mean a colossal stage at a single site. The tradition-dominated IOC would have no problem finding allies in contending that the Olympics would not be the same festival without every athlete and every nation represented in one place and celebrating a common experience.[93]

A better idea is the recommendation to reduce the scope of the Games. By eliminating some events, the huge cost of staging the Olympics would be decreased, thus encouraging more cities in smaller and less politically important nations to bid for the Games. From a political point of view, striking team sports--the most nationalistic of all Olympic competitions--from the Games program would be the most sensible option. Even Coubertin did not favor the inclusion of team sports in the Olympics.[94] Of those presently on the slate, only soccer enjoys an unquestioned avid worldwide following, and soccer competition in the World Cup is far more important than in the Olympic Games.[95] Unsurprisingly, problems of feasibility arise. Since the IOC does not pay the bills for staging the Olympics, it feels little pressure to reduce their size. Federations governing sports not presently on the Olympic agenda are constantly clamoring for inclusion, and the IOC has added synchronized swimming and rhythmic gymnastics for 1984 and tennis and table tennis for 1988. Dropping sports from the Games agenda is unlikely to happen; the Olympics offer prestige in athletic as well as political circles, and it is probable that the IOC would succumb to what would surely be intense lobbying from the officials of any sport threatened with elimination.

Pressure is mounting on the IOC to open the Olympic Games to all competitors, amateur or not. This issue did not spark major controversy in 1984, but the potential for an explosion increases as state-supported athletes from Eastern bloc nations strengthen their domination over what is still called amateur sport.[96] The dilemma about amateurism provides perhaps the best evidence of the IOC's reactionary nature. "For years now," comments Bill Shirley, "amateurism has been as dead as the standing high jump, a fact recognized by everyone on the planet but the IOC."[97] Wealthy gentlemen who view sport as a leisure activity and not as a profession still hold great power within the IOC.

The world has changed, but the IOC has not. In order for Western athletes even to attempt to compete successfully against their Eastern rivals while retaining amateur status, various forms of deferred payments, trust funds, and part-time job opportunities have surfaced. These schemes are rife for potential corruption and athlete exploitation, yet the IOC is less worried about the possibility of graft being exposed than about the impossible preservation of a nineteenth-century ideal. Besides, by opening the Games to amateurs and professionals alike, the IOC would fulfill what is currently just another ideal--Olympic competition among the world's best athletes. In any case, IOC cries about commercializing the Games by paying sportsmen ring hollow. The IOC itself earns money by marketing products with Olympic symbols worldwide and pockets additional profits from the payments of television networks and corporate sponsors.[98] Only hypocrisy triumphs when the athletes--without whom the Games cannot exist-- are the only party that cannot make any money from them.

If one is suspicious of the decidedly skeptical attitude presented here toward Olympic reform, consider the following as the ultimate illustration of the IOC's blind faith in idealism and resistance to meaningful change. The IOC has discussed presenting a resolution to the United Nations that would give official international recognition to the Olympic Games and to the IOC as the body that controls them. One report suggested that the IOC would include provisions that, upon approval of the resolution, "would protect the Olympic Games from boycotts [and] recognize the independence of the national Olympic committees from government control."[99] Both of those provisions are utterly ludicrous. The government of any country in the world--some of which are directly represented on the IOC--can testify that no nation that objects to a U.N. resolution need subscribe to it, and no penalty is assessed for violating any provisions therein. Such is the nature of the United Nations, where either the United States or the Soviet Union can by itself veto any major action considered by the Security Council. The second clause is truly absurd. Most NOCs have not been, are not now, and never will be free of government influence, let alone government domination. If the IOC seriously believes a U.N. resolution can reform the Olympic Games, then IOC members should gather en masse in a time machine and travel to 1928. Assuredly, IOC representatives would have much in common with the signers of the Kellogg-Briand Pact, a 63- nation covenant that outlawed war.

One day after the Soviet Union announced its boycott of the 1984 Olympics, the *Chicago Tribune* editorialized, "If the IOC can hear the death knell of its movement tolling from two ruined Olympics, perhaps it will begin a genuine debate on the reforms needed to resurrect and cleanse the Games."[100] The hint that the IOC can remove politics from the Olympics is misleading; if there is anything this work has tried to demonstrate, it is that sport and politics are inseparable.[101] The IOC could reduce the level of politics in the Games, but only by dramatically changing their structure to diminish their grandeur.[102] The chances are slim, almost nonexistent, that the IOC will take any such action that will decrease the majesty of the Games. However, the call for a "genuine debate" is valid. A legitimate, wide-ranging discussion within the IOC, especially under Samaranch's leadership, might result in the acknowledgment that politics is indeed an Olympic event and the consideration of that factor in future IOC decisions. This type of adaptation to reality, under present conditions, would represent true reform. It might also prevent the Games from suffering a fate increasingly predicted for them: extinction.

All of the suggestions for reform have a common foundation: the conviction that the Olympics are in a sickly state and need prompt healing. These recommendations are so pervasive, in fact, that perhaps we need to stop and consider if we are asking the wrong question. Instead of concerning ourselves with improving the Games, beset as they are with problems, why not terminate the Games and put them out of their misery? We have chronicled a litany of Olympic troubles in Chapters Two and Three, and the evidence presented in this chapter indicates that matters are likely to get worse before they get better. In the face of almost constant adversity, why save the Olympics?

The first and the simplest argument for continuing the Olympic Games is to benefit the world's athletes. "Olympic athlete" is as good as definition as any of the word "pawn." As pointed out in a quote opening Chapter Two and subsequently discussed throughout this work, athletes rank behind politicians, the media, the IOC, commercial sponsors, and just about anyone else involved in the Games in profiting--literally and figuratively--from them. The Olympics provide a grand political forum, but they also provide magnificent competition for and among the world's best athletes. "Even as commercialism permeates the Games and nations use them for political purposes," observes writer Robert Sullivan, "the individual athlete can still strive for excellence."[103]

Second, instead of contending that politics have wounded the Olympics, perhaps mortally, let us argue that the political involvement in and utility of the Games makes them worth preserving. Since the 1900 Paris Games and the 1904 St. Louis Games were both held as sideshows in international expositions, those Olympiads were largely ignored by politicians. It is not coincidental, David Kanin notes, that these were also the least successful Olympiads.[104] Throughout their history, many nations have exploited the political opportunities inherent in the Games. For small countries, participation in Olympic politics and success in Olympic athletic events offer rare moments of publicity and glory with the whole world watching. Global attention is not readily paid to less powerful nations in most other international forums.[105]

Much more important is the political value of the Games to large countries. Samaranch says it is the IOC's duty to "try and convince politicians that to take sport as a hostage for political purposes only serves to create new sources of conflict throughout the world."[106] While this assertion is sometimes valid, Olympic politics, in general, diminish rather than add to global strife. Recall the George Orwell quote that opens this chapter. Olympic "war without shooting" has come to mean far more than the fiercely nationalistic international rivalries inherent in the Games. The Olympic Games are now a full-fledged diplomatic weapon in a country's political arsenal.

The U.S. boycott of the 1980 Moscow Games provides a perfect example. The boycott was a direct response to the Soviet invasion of Afghanistan. Several decades ago, a military reaction might have been in order, but exercising such an option today carries with it the weight of extreme danger in this nuclear era. The boycott conveyed U.S. condemnation of the Soviet action without risking military acceleration or all-out war. The attractiveness of using the Olympics as a political tool is enhanced when other diplomatic strategies are considered. For many countries, maneuvers like imposing economic sanctions and suspending diplomatic relations are often inappropriate, not fiscally prudent, or simply not in a nation's best interest.[107] An Olympic-related political move offers the enticing combination of great exposure with minimal repercussions. As journalist William Oscar Johnson observes:

> Using young Olympians as pawns in these grim games of international politics is a dirty trick, but it costs very little--no weapons, no money to speak of, no brinksmanship, and, most wonderful blessing of all, no lives.[108]

Contemporary political utility, then, is one reason the Olympics should continue, and the vested interest so many world leaders have in maintaining the valuable political forum that is the Olympic Games virtually guarantees their survival for at least the foreseeable future. Ironically, the Games may also be saved through a method the IOC is bound to abhor. Despite the IOC's idealistic rhetoric, the dollar sign has begun to symbolize the Olympics more accurately than the gold medal, and the IOC itself profits from marketing Olympic merchandise. Much of the money today comes from U.S. television networks, and with payment comes power. For instance, with NBC footing about 15 percent of the bill for the 1988 Games, Seoul organizers have changed the times of some competitions so that they can begin during prime viewing time in the United States.[109] The Olympics are literally worth so much to so many parties--broadcasters, corporate sponsors, and the IOC itself among them--that commercialism may be a savior of the Games.

Harry Edwards suggests that the Olympic Games, "as a 19th century Western institution," have been "overrun by the course of complexity of 20th century political events."[110] While Edwards is not incorrect, it is more accurate to state that the Olympics have been shaped--more than overrun--by contemporary politics. Orwell's "war without shooting" description of the Games has never been more accurate than in this nuclear age, and I would contend that quality is an admirable one. If IOC members were to view themselves in the wider role of world citizens, they should be grateful--if only grudgingly--for the Olympic alternative to more perilous political and military strategies. Besides, as the Los Angeles Games showed, political activity need not preclude a successful Olympiad. "By pushing ahead in both 1980 and [1984]," wrote Jerry Kirshenbaum, "the Olympics, for their part, showed that they can at least attempt to transcend politics, even if they can't escape them. And even nonbelievers may draw a measure of spiritual comfort from the knowledge that the Games so far have out-Roman-numeraled World Wars by a lopsided XXIII to II."[111]

I have gone to great lengths in this work to point out the damaging effects of idealism. I do not wish, however, to condemn the general principle of idealism. In the poetry of Robert Browning, "A man's reach must exceed his grasp, or what's a heaven for?" But the contemporary Olympic Games do not represent paradise on Earth. By tempering idealism with realism, the Olympics can be preserved and enhanced. By acknowledging instead of denying political reality, the Olympics will truly reflect their ancient heritage. Present perceptions might paralyze the Games, but peering into the past can indeed provide prologue for a prosperous future.

NOTES

Epigram: George Orwell, as quoted in *Los Angeles Times*, September 25, 1983.

1. *Los Angeles Times*, July 18, 1976. Buckley's comment predates the 1980 U.S. boycott and the 1984 Soviet boycott.
2. Quoted in *Los Angeles Times*, May 13, 1984.
3. Quoted in *Sports Illustrated*, May 21, 1984.
4. Ibid.
5. Quoted in *Los Angeles Times*, August 14, 1984. The

newspaper is the *Basler Zeitung*.

6. *Los Angeles Times*, July 31, 1985.
7. *Los Angeles Times*, June 19, 1985; October 18, 1986.
8. *Sports Illustrated*, August 27, 1985.
9. *Los Angeles Times*, June 19, 1985.
10. Quoted in *Los Angeles Times*, February 22, 1981.
11. Ibid.
12. *Los Angeles Times*, July 28, 1985.
13. *Los Angeles Times*, August 13, 1984.
14. *Los Angeles Times*, September 30, 1984.
15. Quoted in *Los Angeles Times*, July 28, 1985.
16. However, the Seoul Games are unlikely to engender as much nationalism as the Los Angeles Games did. The victory orgy that fanned U.S. nationalistic fires in 1984 will not be a factor in 1988. South Korean athletes are nowhere near as talented as their U.S. counterparts and will probably win very few medals.
17. *Los Angeles Times*, July 28, 1985.
18. Associated Press release, February 24, 1987.
19. *Sports Illustrated*, September 23, 1985.
20. *Los Angeles Times*, April 3, 1983.
21. *Sports Illustrated*, September 23, 1985.
22. *Los Angeles Times*, December 4, 1985.
23. *Los Angeles Times*, March 26, 1986; March 27, 1986.
24. *Los Angeles Times*, December 4, 1985; March 27, 1986.
25. *Los Angeles Times*, October 5, 1986.
26. Edwards (1985); *Los Angeles Times*, August 13, 1984.
27. Edwards (1985).
28. *Los Angeles Times*, August 13, 1984.
29. *Los Angeles Times*, July 28, 1985.
30. *Oakland Tribune*, January 9, 1986.
31. *Los Angeles Times*, August 11, 1984.
32. *Los Angeles Times*, July 10, 1986; July 17, 1986.
33. Quoted in *Los Angeles Times*, July 10, 1986.
34. *Los Angeles Times*, July 3, 1986.
35. Associated Press release, February 12, 1987; *Contra Costa Times*, February 14, 1987.
36. *Chicago Tribune*, December 7, 1986. The three cities are Beijing, Moscow, and the Soviet town of Khabarovsk.
37. Quoted in *Los Angeles Times*, September 30, 1986.
38. *Chicago Tribune*, December 7, 1986.
39. *Los Angeles Times*, September 30, 1984.
40. *Los Angeles Times*, May 18, 1985; October 19, 1986. The figure of 189 dead at Kwangju is an official count. Opposition leaders contend the number is higher.
41. *Los Angeles Times*, March 21, 1986; July 26, 1986.
42. *Los Angeles Times*, May 18, 1985.
43. *Los Angeles Times*, March 11, 1985.
44. *Los Angeles Times*, March 24, 1986.

45. *Los Angeles Times*, March 31, 1986.

46. *Los Angeles Times*, October 31, 1986.

47. *Los Angeles Times*, October 19, 1986. The correspondent is *Los Angeles Times* reporter Sam Jameson.

48. *Los Angeles Times*, October 1, 1985.

49. *Los Angeles Times*, June 1, 1986.

50. *Los Angeles Times*, February 13, 1986; February 14, 1986; July 26, 1986.

51. *Los Angeles Times*, January 15, 1986.

52. *Los Angeles Times*, May 18, 1985; September 5, 1985; March 21, 1986.

53. *Los Angeles Times*, February 13, 1986.

54. *Los Angeles Times*, October 19, 1986.

55. *Los Angeles Times*, February 13, 1986; February 24, 1986.

56. *Los Angeles Times*, March 21, 1986; May 1, 1986.

57. *Los Angeles Times*, May 30, 1986.

58. Quoted in *Los Angeles Times*, March 24, 1986.

59. Quoted in *Los Angeles Times*, March 21, 1986.

60. Quoted in *Los Angeles Times*, September 30, 1986.

61. Quoted in *Los Angeles Times*, January 23, 1986.

62. Quoted in *Los Angeles Times*, March 21, 1986. It is worth noting that the clergy played an influential role in Aquino's takeover in the Philippines.

63. Quoted in *Los Angeles Times*, March 31, 1986.

64. *San Francisco Chronicle*, April 9, 1987; April 18, 1987.

65. *Los Angeles Times*, July 1, 1987.

66. *San Francisco Chronicle*, July 4, 1987.

67. Quoted in *San Francisco Examiner*, July 5, 1987. The speaker is unnamed.

68. *Los Angeles Times*, June 30, 1987.

69. Quoted in *Los Angeles Times*, June 30, 1987.

70. Quoted in *Los Angeles Times*, July 1, 1987.

71. Quoted in *San Francisco Chronicle*, July 1, 1987.

72. Quoted in *Los Angeles Times*, June 29, 1987.

73. Quoted in *Los Angeles Times*, June 30, 1987.

74. *San Francisco Chronicle*, August 26, 1987.

75. Quoted in Associated Press release, February 24, 1987.

76. *Los Angeles Times*, March 12, 1984. For more on South Africa and the Olympics, see pp. 25-26.

77. *Los Angeles Times*, March 16, 1984. The PLO does meet one requirement for admission: membership in five international sports federations. The IOC also stipulates that "the name of an NOC must reflect the territorial extent and tradition of that country" (Olympic Charter, Rule 24). This issue, with regard to the PLO, is at the heart of negotiations for peace in the Middle East. Should the IOC take up a PLO application, the discussion might well be the most politically explosive ever held by that body.

78. *Los Angeles Times*, August 11, 1984; December 3, 1984.

79. Quoted in *Los Angeles Times*, December 3, 1984.

80. Quoted in *Los Angeles Times*, June 2, 1984.

81. LAOOC (1984a), pp. 13-14, and *Los Angeles Times*, September 19, 1981. Congresses are so infrequent that the 1981 meeting was only the eleventh ever held. The first Congress, in 1894, founded the modern Olympic movement (see p. 23). The next Congress is scheduled for 1990. The very rarity of these meetings is a good indication of how little the IOC values outside opinion. (Incidentally, UNESCO is an educational, cultural, and scientific organization under the aegis of the United Nations.)

82. *Los Angeles Times*, September 19, 1981.

83. *Los Angeles Times*, July 25, 1984.

84. *Los Angeles Times*, August 2, 1984.

85. Edwards (1981), p. 240.

86. Edwards (1985).

87. IAAF stands for International Amateur Athletic Foundation, the world governing body for track and field.

88. *Sports Illustrated*, September 14, 1981.

89. *Los Angeles Times*, February 3, 1980.

90. Leiper, p. 114, and Kanin, p. 151.

91. *Los Angeles Times*, September 4, 1981.

92. Leiper, p. 114.

93. In any case, the assumption in this proposal is incorrect. With several host nations rather than one, the possibility of selecting a host country that is politically offensive to one country or another goes up, not down. General political protest at the Games would not decrease, either. Although any one particular site in an Olympics held in multiple locations would not offer as large a local audience for a political viewpoint as would a single-site Games, modern media technology would still instantly transmit political opinions around the world.

94. Henry, p. 8.

95. *Los Angeles Times*, July 29, 1984.

96. For background on the issue of amateur status, see pp. 31-32.

97. *Los Angeles Times*, July 29, 1984.

98. See *Sports Illustrated*, July 16, 1984, and *Los Angeles Times*, May 10, 1984.

99. *Los Angeles Times*, February 5, 1982. See also *Sports Illustrated*, July 16, 1984.

100. Quoted in *Sports Illustrated*, May 21, 1984.

101. Those in need of further persuasion should particularly review Chapter One.

102. Such radical change would require two foci. First, the IOC would have to structure itself and the Games in a framework other than the national one currently employed. Second, the scope of the Games would have to be decreased to the point that they no longer represent a

major international forum, meaning that political statements would gain a greater audience in a different arena.

103. *Sports Illustrated*, August 27, 1984.

104. Kanin, p. ix.

105. The emerging black African nations best exemplify these uses. See pp. 25-26, 58-60.

106. Quoted in *Los Angeles Times*, May 21, 1984.

107. Again, 1980 provides a perfect example. Although U.S. allies did not fully back the U.S. boycott, the Carter administration received far greater support for the boycott than for its other responses to the Soviet invasion of Afghanistan, which included a grain embargo, restrictions on cultural exchanges, and curbs on the export of high-technology equipment to the Soviet Union.

108. *Sports Illustrated*, May 21, 1984.

109. *Sports Illustrated*, September 23, 1985.

110. Edwards (1984), p. 50.

111. *Sports Illustrated*, July 18, 1984. While Los Angeles did host the Games of the XXIII Olympiad, there have been only 20 actual Olympic competitions. World War I forced the cancellation of the 1916 Games, and World War II did the same for the 1940 and 1944 Games. Each four-year period, dating from Athens in 1896, is counted as an Olympiad regardless of whether the Games are actually held.

Bibliography

BOOKS

Coakley, Jay. *Sport in Society: Issues and Controversies.*
St. Louis: C. V. Mosby Co., 1982.
Coleman, James. "Athletics in High School." In George Sage,
ed., *Sport and American Society*. Reading, MA: Addison-
Wesley, 1974.
Douskou, Iris, ed. *The Olympic Games*. Athens: Ekdotike
Athenon S.A., 1976.
Edwards, Harry. *The Struggle That Must Be*. New York:
Macmillan, 1980.
Edwards, Harry. "Crisis in the Modern Olympic Movement." In
Jeffrey Segrave and Donald Chu, eds., *Olympism*.
Champaign, IL: Human Kinetics, 1981.
Espy, Richard. *The Politics of the Olympic Games*. Berkeley:
University of California Press, 1981.
Finley, M. I., and H. W. Pleket. *The Olympic Games: The
First Thousand Years*. New York: Viking Press, 1980.
Greenfield, Jeff. *The Real Campaign: How the Media Missed
the Story of the 1980 Campaign*. New York: Summit Books,
1980.
Grenier, H., and L. Gridley. *Olympic Games Old and New*.
Rivera, CA: The American Printers, 1932.
Guttmann, Allen. *The Games Must Go on: Avery Brundage and
the Olympic Movement*. New York: Columbia University
Press, 1984.
Hazan, Baruch. *Olympic Sports and Propaganda Games*. New
Brunswick, NJ: Transaction Books, 1982.
Henry, Bill. *An Approved History of the Olympic Games*. New
York: G. P. Putnam's Sons, 1976.
Kanin, David. *A Political History of the Olympic Games*.
Boulder, CO: Westview Press, 1981.
Leiper, Jean. "Political Problems in the Olympic Games." In
Jeffrey Segrave and Donald Chu, eds., *Olympism*.
Champaign, IL: Human Kinetics, 1981.
Lucas, John. "The Genesis of the Modern Olympic Games." In
Jeffrey Segrave and Donald Chu, eds., *Olympism*.
Champaign, IL: Human Kinetics, 1981.
Mandell, Richard. *The Nazi Olympics*. New York: Macmillan,
1977.
Mandell, Richard. *Sport: A Cultural History*. New York:
Columbia University Press, 1984.
Michener, James. *Sports in America*. New York: Random House,
1976.
Neft, David, et al. *The Sports Encyclopedia: Baseball*. New
York: Grosset and Dunlap, 1981.

Osterhoudt, Robert. "Capitalist and Socialist
    Interpretations of Modern Amateurism: An Essay on the
    Fundamental Difference." In Jeffrey Segrave and Donald
    Chu, eds., *Olympism*. Champaign, IL: Human Kinetics, 1981.
Riordan, James. *Soviet Sport*. Oxford: Basil Blackwell,
    1980.
Sage, George, ed. *Sport and American Society*. Reading, MA:
    Addison-Wesley, 1974.
Schaap, Dick. *An Illustrated History of the Olympics*. New
    York: Alfred A. Knopf, 1975.
Toohey, Dale, and Kristine Warning. "Nationalism:
    Inevitable and Incurable?" In Jeffrey Segrave and Donald
    Chu, eds., *Olympism*. Champaign, IL: Human Kinetics, 1981.

NEWSPAPERS, MAGAZINES, AND JOURNALS

Chicago Tribune, December 7, 1986.
Contra Costa Times, February 14, 1987.
Edwards, Harry. "Perspectives on Olympic Sportpolitics:
    1968-1984." In *Black Law Journal*. Los Angeles: UCLA
    School of Law, spring 1984.
Los Angeles Times, 1976-1987.
Newsweek, July 26, 1982.
Oakland Tribune, January 9, 1986.
San Francisco Chronicle, March 18, 1985; April 9, 1987;
    April 18, 1987; July 1, 1987; July 4, 1987; August 26,
    1987.
San Francisco Examiner, March 17, 1985; July 5, 1987.
Sports Illustrated, 1980-1985.

OLYMPIC MATERIALS

Los Angeles Olympic Organizing Committee (LAOOC). *Olympic
    Countdown: 200 Days to Go* (1984a).
Los Angeles Olympic Organizing Committee (LAOOC). *Media
    Guide Handbook for Press, Radio, Television Journalists*
    (1984b).
Los Angeles Olympic Organizing Committee (LAOOC). *Games of
    the XXIII Olympiad: Opening Ceremonies* (1984c, official
    program).
Los Angeles Olympic Organizing Committee (LAOOC). *Official
    Olympic Souvenir Program* (1984d).
Los Angeles Olympic Organizing Committee (LAOOC). "Los
    Angeles Attendance Reaches 5,797,923." August 13, 1984
    (1984e, press release).
LAOOC Alumni Organization. "Fanfare." February 1985
    (newsletter).
Press Commission of the Chinese Olympic Committee (COC).
    China and the Olympics (1984a).

Press Commission of the Chinese Olympic Committee (COC). *China's Contemporary Sports* (1984b).
United States Olympic Committee (USOC). *The Olympian*. July/August 1984.

OTHER SOURCES

Associated Press news releases. February 12, 1987; February 24, 1987.
Edwards, Harry. Lecture, University of California. September 1, 1983.
Edwards, Harry. Interview. December 3, 1985.
"Olympic Report." KALX Radio, July 27, 1984.
"Olympics Without the Soviets." *Nightline*, ABC-TV, May 8, 1984.

Index

About the Author

Bill Shaikin is a San Francisco Bay Area sports journalist. He both worked on the staff of and reported on the 1984 Los Angeles Games. He is a 1985 Phi Beta Kappa graduate of the University of California, Berkeley.